IT'S UP TO YOU

IT'S UP TO YOU

Learn Ten Powerful Leadership Practices

Craig Miller

ISBN-13: 9780692062647
ISBN-10: 0692062645

Table of Contents

Preface

Ten years ago, when I decided to leave the corporate world, it felt like I was jumping off a cliff. I've done some pretty scary and risky things in my career and in my life. This was by far the biggest—not only because I was starting my own business after working in someone else's business my whole career but also because my business wasn't clear. It wasn't like I was an architect or a dentist starting my own practice. I was trying something that I'd never done professionally before, and it all felt a little bit like the circus to my family, my wife, and her family. So it felt like I was standing on the edge of a cliff, wind in my face, terror running through me. But I jumped.

I went for it, and at the time I had this fantasy that once I got the company profitable and working, I was done. And I learned quickly that when you have the courage to jump like this, the world sees, "We have a jumper," and it asks you to do it again. So constantly, since starting my business ten years ago, I've been faced with new opportunities to let go of what's easy and try something that's unknown, that's challenging, that may not work. I've been constantly learning and making mistakes, and it seems like the more I do that, the more I'm challenged to keep going.

Since then, I have stayed committed to learning and growth. This book—a scary jump in itself—is simply me sharing what I have learned along the journey. To those of you who are science and fact-based people—which a lot of my clients are—this is not meant to be the absolute truth. This is a compilation of my own observations, my own learning, and the observations and learning of hundreds of clients. After ten years of observation and learning with top leadership from many of the Fortune 500 companies and one year of writing, my promise to you is that by spending a few hours reading (maybe during a flight), you will walk away not only having learned better ways to lead, but even more importantly, you will have a few very tangible practices to put into action tomorrow. And I hope it helps you become a better leader and a more satisfied person.

When I set out to write a book, I had this fantasy of telling all my clients that I was shutting down my business for three months, renting a beach house, and getting a bottle of scotch so I could do nothing but write. But I remembered pretty quickly that I never liked the beach, I don't drink, and I don't even like to write. And so I found Melinda Copp, and we've worked together and partnered on this for a year. It's been an amazing experience, and the book would otherwise still be a fantasy. My ability to ask for help has made this book happen.

Craig's book *It's Up to You: Learn Ten Powerful Leadership Practices* takes a big step toward illuminating a very dark corner of our current world—leadership. The state of our world today is crying for authentic and effective leadership. We need this corner to be illuminated and made accessible so we can develop the leader within each of us.

Leadership is a field where we admire examples and get nuggets of wisdom from those who are accomplished. But discussing leadership is almost always anecdotal with tips and techniques. It may be an interesting story, but we are always left with this question: What do *I* do? Leadership is a performance art and cannot be understood with only concepts. It must be a field of actions, skills, and results. Craig's approach provides exactly this needed perspective. He reveals key actions and skills and ways to make them work that are essential for the effective leader, manager, professional, or person who creates a future with others—and that includes all of us.

It's Up to You provides more than a set of techniques. This perspective is based on a solid foundation that provides a coherent answer to the often-avoided question: What is leadership? This answer includes a fundamental understanding of human beings, action, value, and coordination that we call generative because it reveals the actions we take that generate these outcomes. But this is not theoretical—it's a field of action and results.

The lessons in this book come from Craig's many years of supporting leaders and leadership teams as they overcame the common and recurring breakdowns that occur over and over again in our culture's leadership blind spots. These strategies will elevate your impact, improve your team's performance, and put your energy into valuable outcomes rather than the interpersonal challenges that arise from the blind spots.

Craig walks the talk because his results are the results of others. I've been privileged to watch Craig on his leadership journey and see him face the leadership challenges, face the successes and failures, face himself, and engage in the path of practice to continually learn and grow. He practiced with me for a number of years early in his journey, and he took every question and perplexity as his target for continuing exploration and learning. I remember him asking why in many of our practices, until the light turned on and he saw it as unavoidable and crucial. Since then, Craig has developed his own voice and forged his own path with his continued exploration. By illuminating the path in this book, Craig has shown us how we must engage to be effective in our leadership journey.

As in any performance art, skill develops with practice. Practice is the key to your impact, your growth, and the value you create. Today too many people want the quick fix, the tips and techniques, rather than the real answer for developing powerful leadership skills and effective teams. How many years of practice does it take to become an excellent athlete, lawyer, doctor, or high performer in any field? Leadership is no different, except that the path of practice has been unclear. Craig's gift is showing you essential steps on the path.

Leadership has commonly been described as a set of actions disconnected from the leader's full life journey and the journeys of those affected by that leader's leadership. We are not just "leading" when we lead. We are also living a life with others. We are creating a future and the actions to realize it with others. When we do it with care, and take care of what we care about, leadership can generate a good life for us and the people around us. That illumination gives you new room for design in your life and career.

Enjoy your exploration with Craig, and may it be one step of many in your leadership journey.

Bob Dunham
December 2017

Introduction

In times of change learners will inherit the earth while those attached to their old certainties will find themselves beautifully equipped to deal with a world that no longer exists.

ERIC HOFFER

What does great leadership mean? What does it look like? I work with people in leadership who are very successful. They graduated at the top of the class, have been promoted numerous times, and keep getting more and more responsibility at work. The companies they work for see their potential, and from the outside it may look like they've got everything together. But most of the time, many leaders are just doing the best they can at the whole leadership game without really understanding what it's about. And most of my clients, when they go home at night, can look around and see everything they've worked for and always wanted—the house, the family, the lifestyle. But despite their accomplishments, something seems to be hanging there in the way, preventing them from succeeding at the highest level and leaving them feeling dissatisfied. This happens because leaders, in general, aren't spending enough time truly leading.

This problem is, in part, situational. Companies don't make managers from people who have studied or practiced the management of human beings. A master's in business administration doesn't actually cover management and leadership. They learn about finance, marketing, profit and loss, and how businesses work. Rarely do people learn how to create a team or manage other people. And people get pulled up into management the first time, not because they are good managers or leaders, but because they're really good at getting stuff done. They're good performers. This is universal all over the world; I can talk about it in Colombia, in Japan, in Germany, in the United States, anywhere I go, and people nod their heads. So when rising leaders get more responsibility and find themselves in stressful situations, they tend to keep doing what has always made them successful in the past: they do more work. Why? Because no one ever taught them any different, and they don't know how to improve. Further complicating matters, the system itself needs an overhaul.

Most companies out there still use what's known as command and control. The boss tells the worker what to do and how to do it and makes sure they're doing it right. And the worker is supposed to obey. The goal in command and control is compliance. This model was created in the industrial revolution, and it made sense then. The problem is that—even when everyone says, "Yes, ma'am"—no one's really bought in. There's a difference between compliance and commitment. Great leadership happens when the followers are committed. They are not doing their work because someone told them to, but because they understand and care about the end game, and are bringing their talent, creativity, and best efforts to producing that desired outcome.

Lack of leadership is epidemic in command and control management. It manifests as micromanaging, leaders trying to be all-powerful, telling other people what to do. In a matrix organization, where there are lots of verticals and horizontals, people have multiple stakeholders. And it's not always clear who is really in charge or how to take care of everyone, including yourself. People get multiple, contradictory requests and all sorts of wacky stuff happens all day long. But nobody steps up and says, "I own this. Here's what it looks like for me to be totally satisfied." Nobody asks people what they can commit to; instead they tell them what to do. And no one understands why he or she is doing it.

The amount of suffering, animosity, bad politics, and shit that happens in these organizations always bothers me. People don't talk to each other. People work for weeks on projects only to have the boss swoop in at the last minute and take credit for everything. This stuff happens all the time. Why? Command and control filters down from the top. The executives can't shoulder all the blame, because even they have shareholders and other people they have to answer to. But most companies would be a lot more profitable if leaders were more empowering than controlling. These changes affect work life for everyone involved, and in a global company with thousands of employees and millions of customers, shifting away from command and control could change the world.

We see studies all the time indicating low motivation in the workforce and talent not being tapped. We're not getting the juice out of our people, and it's a leadership issue. It's not the people doing the work. But we're still applying an old model, which doesn't allow for creativity or innovation. The boss is supposed to know all the answers and tell people what to do. The reason that's happening is because we're not taught anything different; most of the time we're all just copying what our boss did before us. And although the people in the executive suite are in the best position to get rid of command and control forever, you can do better and create change no matter where you are.

The best definition of leadership I've ever heard is declaring a future that other people will commit to. When President Kennedy said the United States would have a man on the moon by the end of the decade, even though he didn't know exactly how we'd get there, he was declaring his vision of the future. Leaders need vision—a goal for the future—and you're not leading until other people commit to it. This definition is helpful to many leaders—beginners and those with years of experience—because it's simple and it reveals what leadership is not.

Leading is not managing. It is about seeing and sharing the vision and then engaging the promises of others to make that vision a measurable outcome. Management is the day-to-day making and managing of promises, which end up producing the vision of the leader. But when you're just doing the best you can, seeing that difference is hard. For example, I worked with a client who was an effective manager. He went to all the meetings, read all the e-mails, and got involved in everything. When he asked me for help, the feedback he'd been getting from his superiors was, "You're not being strategic enough, and you're not seeing the big picture. We think you're capable of that." I worked with this client for months, helping him learn new practices, let go, empower other people, and get out of the weeds so he could step up more. Then we started a call one day, and I asked how he was.

"Horrible," he said. So I asked him what was going on, and he explained, "I'm convinced that I've lost my edge. That they're phasing me out. I'm not being invited to half the meetings I used to go to. My inbox is down sixty percent. And I don't even know what I'm doing here anymore or why I'm supposed to be here. I think I'm getting fired."

He couldn't see me through the phone, but I was smiling the whole time. He wasn't getting fired; he was succeeding at exactly what we'd been working on. And it scared the crap out of him because he felt like his job was to have his hand in every bucket, to be in every meeting, to be giving his input all over the place. You can't lead if you're busy doing all of that.

Leadership—great leadership—is not about being busy or being involved in everything. Being a leader doesn't mean doing the work, it doesn't mean attending every meeting. And so in my client's case, he started playing that leadership game, and of course he wasn't as busy. Welcome to leadership. That's the whole point. You want to get to a place where your calendar has blank spaces. You're not back to back every single day. Because if you want to be a great leader, you can't spend all your time managing tasks. You need space in your calendar to talk to your team members and to coach those who are struggling. You have to have spontaneous conversations with the people you're leading. And you have to lift up your chin metaphorically and see what's coming next. Unfortunately, many people in corporate leadership fail to do this.

TAKING THE LEAD

When I work with teams in organizations, I walk in as an outsider and say, "How do you win the game that you are playing right now?" But they often can't answer the question. They don't know the game. What does success look like? If you don't know, then how do you know if you are doing well? Someone has to be clear on where the organization is going.

When a leader is unclear on his or her vision, it creates waste for people who are doing the work. I once heard Yves Morieux from the Boston Consulting Group talk about how up to 60 percent of work that's done in organizations is actually done, undone, and redone. People are doing stuff. Then they're undoing it, and then they're redoing it because it wasn't aligned with a clear goal from the beginning. That creates tremendous waste, distrust, and a decrease in motivation. Many times, because the leader is afraid to tell somebody to undo what they did and redo it, he ends up just doing it himself on a Friday night.

Imagine you're in a theater watching a ballet. Down on the floor, the dancers are dancing; the work is being done. But up in the balcony, the director has a view of the whole show; he's taking in the big picture and making adjustments so everything works toward the overall goal. As leaders, we need to be on the dance floor and in the balcony. You need to do both, and you need to go back and forth. If you spend too much time on the dance floor, you're down there in the weeds, working hard, but then no one's steering everyone toward the goal. This is where most leaders spend most of their time. But you can't be an effective leader if you don't take many moments to check in and observe from a higher perspective. What conversations are missing or not being had? Are my team and I spending time on activities aligned to the end game? Is the end game clear for everyone? Having a captain of the ship focused on the horizon and watching the team from above adds immense value. That's the only way to see what is missing and what is off. At the same time, you can't lose touch with the people you're leading. You have to listen and understand and anticipate their needs. You have to help them overcome their challenges. You have to have conversations and create a safe environment where they can be honest with you.

So what can you do to become a great leader? Unfortunately, there is no magic pill. When my brother was in college, he lost a lot of weight one summer. And when he went back to school, everyone asked him his secret. He told them all, "I ate less and exercised more." No one liked that answer because it was so simple and so unexciting. But change doesn't happen overnight, and leadership is the same way. You don't become a good leader by going to hear a motivational speaker or by reading ten books on leadership. Otherwise we'd all be professional golfers.

You become a good leader the same way you become a good dancer or a good guitar player: by practicing. Improving your leadership skills is not about doing it once; it's about creating an ongoing practice that builds over time. As the Greek poet Archilochus once described, in times of stress we do not rise to our potential; we lower to the level of our practice. In other words, when the shit hits the fan, you're going to go back to what you've always done. So what's the level of your practice? Leadership is a performance art; you have to practice if you want to be good at it. Eventually, when it does get tough, the new practice feels natural and your body does that instead.

Often when I work with clients, they resist new practices and change in general for fear of losing their edge or their talent. For example, they feel that if they focus on pushing back and saying no, they will lose their ability to empathize and take care of others. I help them build courage to try, and every time they see that, they realize what they have practiced for years does not go away. They simply build a larger repertoire.

I once worked with a client who told me, "If I had more time, I could work on this leadership stuff."

So I asked, "What's your job?"

"Well, I'm the chief financial officer," he said. "My job is to make sure that the financials are sound in our company."

This was what he'd always done to be successful, but he was wrong. His job was to lead a team of people to make sure the financials were sound. But it is so hard to think about leading because we get lost in the stuff that we're trained to do. But if you're the chief financial officer, you can't work on reports. Your job is to constantly be listening to your people and knowing who needs help, where their next challenge is, how can you help them, and what they are missing. Your job is to get the very best out of your team and your team members' teams. Doing all of that well—being a great leader—isn't easy. But the good news is that you don't have to have all the answers.

One of my teachers, Bob Dunham, says, "Awareness brings choice." If you see the problem, now you have a choice. My goal for this book is to shake people up—to show you what you perhaps haven't been able to see on your own—and to give you practices that you can use to create change and become a better leader.

GIVE YOURSELF PERMISSION TO BE A BEGINNER

Have you ever had a moment when everyone in the room seems to know what they're doing except for you? Getting promoted into leadership is exciting, but it can also be pretty scary. And although it might feel like you're supposed to already know how to do it well, most people don't. Leadership has to be learned and practiced. Many leaders—even experienced ones—have never practiced good listening, effective communication, empathy, or other essential leadership skills.

As counterintuitive as this may sound, oftentimes becoming a better leader means admitting that you don't know what you're doing. The best leader I've ever worked with—I remember it perfectly—showed up for our first meeting and said, "I know we need to end up here, but I have no idea how to get there. Can you help me?" I've never had so much fun working with someone because it was the first time that, instead of getting a task and being told what to do, I was included in the larger challenge. That person was tapping into my abilities and creativity to work with my colleagues on actually solving a bigger issue, and the leader didn't presume he knew all the answers. I've told so many people about that leader, and they get it. But we live in a world where admitting you don't know what you're doing is seen as weak. We're supposed to know everything, right? Wrong.

A few years ago, I worked with a leader who was constantly getting feedback from her superiors about micromanaging and not listening enough to her people. We looked at what was happening, did some work, and found that this leader had learned and had been leading by telling people what to do, solving problems, and then moving on as fast as possible. Not only is that too much work for the leader, it wasn't empowering the people at all, and they were complaining. So we worked on not interrupting, getting better at listening, and asking more questions instead of telling people what to do. Then after some practice, this leader sat down with the team and told them she was working on these skills. This, in my opinion, was a courageous move because these people had been complaining about her. Not only did the leader say to the team, "I'm going to practice listening more to you guys," but she also said, "I'm probably not going to be very good at it, so please be patient. And I really appreciate your feedback." The team respected her a lot more for being open like that, the team stepped up, and the situation improved.

In a world changing as fast as ours is today, when people try to hold on to what they know because it's comfortable and safe and that's the way they learned it, they limit themselves and the level of satisfaction in life they can achieve. Give yourself a break. You don't know everything—no one does—and you're not supposed to. By giving yourself permission to be a beginner, you can move beyond all the habits that haven't been working and start building a leadership practice that gives you the space you need to lead, fosters teamwork, inspires and motivates your team, and shifts everything around you toward success.

If you want to be a great leader, you have to get the team to work as one. This is every leader's challenge, and it's often the source of dissatisfaction as well. Unfortunately, leadership can't be accomplished by following a set of steps. There is no system. But I believe we are what we practice.

Throughout the book I'll refer to generative practices, which are generative because they generate a different future. For example, everywhere in the world, companies and leaders and teams are saying, "We need more collaboration." Although we all know what collaboration is, how do we do that? A generative practice for collaboration might be asking for help and offering to help others. It's generative because it's something everyone on the team can start doing right away. You can put that on your to-do list. And if you look around the office, you can actually see people doing it. This is how to build a future of collaboration. Any one of the generative practices I describe can be added to your list.

Creating a profound shift takes time, and changing means taking an honest look in the mirror. It means each leader must put people first, model the behaviors you want to see, take the risk, and let people build the commitments from the bottom up. And it often means giving some attention to something other than the ninety-day number you have to hit. The amazing thing about changing your behaviors is that soon things start to finally come together. The team works better. You feel less stressed and less overwhelmed. And finally, the dissatisfaction dissipates. So let's get started.

1

Learn to Say No

Most leaders I encounter live at some level of overwhelm—whether they just have a lot going on or they're struggling to keep up. No one says, "My work and life are completely balanced, and I feel like I'm in control." I don't hear it ever. When I meet leaders and talk to them about their experiences at work, I hear comments like, "It always feels like I'm trying to stay afloat." And, "I know I'm capable of more, but I can't seem to step up." They often change jobs or roles in search of a better fit, thinking things will improve. But do they? These struggles are pervasive among corporate leadership. Further complicating the problem, people who are really good at what they do sometimes have trouble admitting they're dissatisfied or that something isn't working. And oftentimes these people are working at such a senior level, the stakes are really high. The higher up you are, the farther you could fall, and the more you think you should be good. Even sharing their feelings with others—spouses, friends, colleagues—feels risky. How could such a high performer get stuck? How could someone who has everything feel dissatisfied? It happens all the time, but most people feel they can't share that with anyone.

Leaders tend to fall on a personality spectrum. On one end are people who are power and control freaks with a dictatorial presence, bordering on narcissistic bullies. Leaders like this are incredibly effective in the short term. They get shit done. But this behavior ultimately does not encourage followship. People don't like working for them. They don't feel like they have the ability to own anything themselves. They don't feel empowered, and they certainly don't take the initiative. Because this narcissistic type of leader is so encompassing, it's like there's no space for anybody else. And so the leader ends up overextended and overwhelmed.

The other extreme is the incredibly empathetic, nice leaders who are great listeners and really good at connecting with people. However, they struggle with handling conflict, saying no, and having tough conversations, which are essential leadership qualities. People won't trust them or follow them. People who work for this type of leader often get frustrated because decisions are not being made, they don't feel protected by the politics and games that exist in organizations, and ultimately they don't feel as safe. And unfortunately, these leaders end up doing all the work themselves. So they're overburdened and overextended.

Everyone falls somewhere in that spectrum, but oftentimes the closer you are to either extreme, the more dissatisfied and overwhelmed you are. Dissatisfied doesn't mean depressed, demotivated, or totally unfulfilled. When successful people feel dissatisfied, it's often because they have something in their work or life that keeps coming up and biting them. As a result, they're not spending enough time with their family. They can never catch up because they can't get the people who work for them to actually do the work. This dissatisfaction often overshadows everything in life. It feels like life is living you, instead of you living life.

When I was working in my corporate career, my wife named my dissatisfaction: "Sunday depression." It happened every week—I'd enjoy my weekend until Sunday night when I realized I had to be at work the following morning. My energy and mood changed enough for my wife to notice and name it because, more than anything, I did not want to go. Now, I want to put things in perspective. Was I in this horrible slave-driving environment? Of course not. I was doing an executive job, making great money. From the outside it looked amazing. I was leading a team. I was succeeding. I was getting promoted. But I dreaded it.

Why? Because I didn't feel like my boss understood me. I constantly felt that I had to sell my soul to get the work done. I was going against my own values, even though I didn't really understand what those were yet. It was like I was so busy trying to succeed that along the way I forgot who I was and what mattered. And at the same time, I didn't really have relationships with my team, and I didn't know how to build stronger ones. I avoided difficult conversations with people who worked for me, and I had trouble asking them to do more. So I ended up taking on too much work. It was just easier to do it myself than explain and delegate and trust. And so the end story was I didn't see my family and I was overwhelmed at work.

When someone is overwhelmed at the highest level, they are at risk of burning out. I hear all the time about people who end up stepping down, or worse, suffering a heart attack or other stress-related sickness. But overwhelm starts long before that. And it's a huge part of what happens all the time in organizations. The mood that comes with overwhelm is where things get tricky. For some it involves paralysis, for others it is about retreating and hoping that things will take care of themselves. However people react to stress, the old stories show up (I am not good enough. I will not figure this out. Why does this always happen to me?), and we lose our sense of choice, power, and the calm needed to actually move through the stress.

Overwhelm is simply promising results that are beyond your capacity to fulfill. While I've seen people try to take on overwhelm by getting better at time management, using a better calendar, or hiring a personal assistant, the real key that sits between people's ability to manage overwhelm is the capacity to say no.

SAYING NO IS ESSENTIAL

Learning to say no can eliminate overwhelm. The problem with saying no is that we feel like we can't. In corporate culture, it seems we believe no is not a possible answer. We have to do what we're asked, right? Otherwise the boss will be angry.

But there's a way to say no while you're still trying to take care of the person. When you say no, what you're saying is, "I'd rather not say yes to you and then not fulfill." If you know there's no way you can get something done, then be honest. And instead of saying no and walking away, bring a counteroffer. For example, "No, I can't have it to you by Tuesday, but I can absolutely have it to you by Thursday. Is that okay?" Most of the time the answer will be, "Sure, that's fine." It's actually easier to build trust with a person who occasionally pushes back and says no. That way their yes means more. When I was at the end of my corporate career, I would say to my people, "Please know that saying no to me is not only okay, it's desired."

If you consider that spectrum of leader personalities, the ones who get the most benefit from learning to say no are the ones who are highly empathetic and avoid conflict. I've worked with some leaders who are really good at pushing back, but there's a huge population of leaders who need to learn how to walk into conflict.

For example, as part of my work with a CEO, I personally talked to the members of his team in a 360-degree interview process (during this process I interview my client's key stakeholders, peers, and the people who report to him for a full picture of the situation). What I found out was, as amazing as this leader was at his job—he was smart and generous—he was always looking for ways to keep everybody in harmony and getting along and avoiding difficult conversations. When I said to his direct report, "What's the cost for you? Why does that matter?" his response was, "Because I don't know where I stand. I never get feedback from my boss. I'm dying for him to say not only what I'm doing well but what I'm not doing well."

Another comment was, "He doesn't say no. I'll bring a project that I think might have a possibility, and I can see in his body language in three seconds that he believes it's not going to happen. It's not the right project. But he won't actually say it." This creates waste because this person goes back to his team and starts working on something that's not going to work out. The interviewee said, "I wish that if he sees what I don't see, he'd just say it." When a leader can't say no or have the difficult conversations, it creates lack of respect, lack of trust, and waste in the organization.

So how do you fix that? How do you learn to say no? You don't have to walk into your boss's office, terrified, and say, "No, I'm not going to work on that." You can start small to build the muscle. For example, I had a client who had a really hard time with confrontation, saying no, and having difficult conversations. So we talked about starting small and one of his big victories came when he was having lunch in a restaurant. The server brought him the wrong sandwich, and instead of just eating it—which is what he normally would have done—he sent it back and asked them to remake it. For him, this was difficult, but it flexed that muscle, and he started to see that the world wouldn't implode because he pushed back and said no. So start small. This weekend when your spouse suggests meeting friends, if you don't feel like it, then take a deep breath and say, "You know what? I'd really rather not." And see what happens.

I once read about a Zen master who said that he meditates for a half an hour every day, and on busy days he meditates for an hour. Although counterintuitive, the key to managing overwhelm starts with a really deep breath and the ability to go slow to go fast. Have you ever noticed that when a soccer team is losing one nil, the coach always comes out and instructs the players to slow down, relax, and come back to their game plan. The next time you feel that wave of overwhelm in your body, don't resist it. Notice it, and take a really deep breath to regain your control and power.

LET OTHERS STEP UP

Giving people on your team the space to step up and take responsibility is another important way to ease overwhelm. When you're overwhelmed, it's so hard to imagine taking the time to work with a team when you could just do it yourself. But when you struggle to let go and allow others to step up, you won't get much time with your family and overwhelm will inevitably compound. When I do 360-degree interviews, so many times I hear the leader saying, "I'm exhausted. I'm overwhelmed. I'm not seeing my family, and I'm frustrated." And I hear the team saying, "I wish he would just get out of the way more because we could do so much more." It's a vicious circle.

When I work with teams on this, I ask them, "What is it that you, the team need from this leader, to enable you to take more responsibility? To take more ownership?" Their responses always describe a leader who is holding on too tight. In this case, the leader and the team have to work on the problem together to answer the questions: What does the team need from the leader to have more space and more ability to do things your way and take more responsibility? And what does the team need to bring, promise, and learn so the leader feels comfortable letting go? Both the team and the leader have to be having this conversation.

ELIMINATING OVERWHELM

Many people struggle to say no. It takes courage even when you have a counteroffer. We feel like saying no will let the other person down or create conflict. We don't want to offend anyone or be in uncomfortable situations, and then we avoid having those conversations with people. We keep saying yes because our deepest fear is not fulfilling our promises, not being trustworthy, and not being seen as valuable. But by not having the capacity to say no, we take on too much and can't deliver anyway. For me, because I wasn't willing to let the other person down and lose my reputation as the good guy, the only possible solution, which I lived through in my corporate career, was that I spent Friday nights working on Excel spreadsheets, missing my kids' games because I had a project to finish, and working sixty to seventy hours a week to make it happen. Learning how to push back, how to make counteroffers, and how to walk into that conflict and say no will alleviate overwhelm and diminish your late nights at the office.

2

Learn to Ask for Help

Leaders who struggle to ask for help become super performers because they put themselves under tremendous pressure to do it all alone. And that amount of pressure can be overwhelming.

I often meet with leaders—especially at the beginning of our work—and they look almost shell-shocked. They are sitting there with the weight of the world on their shoulders, often experiencing what I would call a mood of resignation, like, "Okay, I'm going to work with a coach, and we're going to try something. But I don't think anything is going to work, because I don't even have time to think about what's wrong, let alone do something about it." That's how people show up. And one reason for this is that they often have a story getting in the way. They actually believe that they have to do everything, hold everything, own everything themselves. And until they know what the right path is, what the right answer is, nothing can happen, which creates not only overwhelm for themselves but a bottleneck for the team and the rest of the organization. Leaders who don't learn how to ask for help completely limit their ability to create bigger promises, to make a bigger impact, and, at the end of the day, to lead. Because if the only answer is that it has to be me sitting in the middle of everything, we're not going to get very big.

Asking for help is different than delegation. Delegation is about trust, and it means asking someone to do a task, like this: "I'm working on this incredibly important project for our boss, and I need you to create a spreadsheet for me." The most challenging part of that is whether or not you can trust the person will do what you've asked. Asking for help, on the other hand, is sitting down with the person who works for you and saying, "Our boss has actually trusted us, me, with this incredibly important project, and I'm not sure how we can do this. I'm wondering if you can help me figure this out." Asking for help is about vulnerability; it's about admitting that I can't get there without you. We're afraid of that. It's uncomfortable, and so we avoid it.

Why is it so hard to ask for help? In part because we were taught that leaders are supposed to be perfect human beings with an answer for everything. And we believe that asking for help means we're failing. But when we dig past these ideas and fears, oftentimes we find the impostor syndrome.

THE IMPOSTOR SYNDROME

The impostor syndrome is a huge underlying problem for high-achieving people. It means you're unable to internalize and appreciate your own accomplishments, so the story you tell yourself sounds like this: "I hope nobody figures out I never should have made it this far." And we tell ourselves, "Since I really shouldn't have gotten this far, if I start asking for help they're going to discover me." It's almost like we're afraid that if everyone notices we don't have it all under control, everything will fall apart. Like I'm going to lose this whole house of cards that I've built; it's all going to come crumbling down. This is almost always not the case.

Again, we don't get promoted into leadership because we're good leaders. We get promoted because we're good performers. It's like being a salesperson, and then all of a sudden, because you're such a good salesperson, someone says, "Oh, you should manage salespeople." Now your job is not to sell, but to manage, and that's a totally different skill set. Even though we may feel hesitation, no one says, "I don't feel qualified for this," because it's incredibly motivating and exciting that someone's paying you more and calling you a manager. So everyone goes, "Great." Fifteen years later, you feel like you've been faking it to make it the whole time. The real problem with the impostor syndrome is that these people tend to walk on eggshells and play it really safe, never fully allowing their power and talent and creativity and passion to show up.

First, we have to realize that a lot of us feel this way. I mentioned the two ends of the leadership personality spectrum, where one is the pleaser who avoids conflict and wants harmony, and at the other end is the dictator who wants control—well, they both live in fear. A lot of the people, at the end of the day, truly believe that they're not enough. No matter how accomplished or how successful, nothing's ever good enough. When we understand that, deep down, we all feel like that, we can be more empathetic and compassionate toward others. And most importantly, we have to be more compassionate with ourselves.

Consider your accomplishments. A lot of people never acknowledge their progress—they never take a second to pat themselves on the back for all the hard work they've put into reaching a milestone or goal. They're too busy focusing on their own shortcomings. Simply taking a minute to acknowledge and appreciate how far you've come can have an amazing effect.

Overcoming the impostor syndrome and that nagging fear means getting clear on who you actually are. Are you a person controlled by fear? Is that who you want to be? I bet not.

HOW TO ASK FOR HELP

Traditionally, people believe the leader should never be vulnerable. It's weakness. But vulnerability is where we actually show up authentically as we are, and this is where human beings connect. And as a leader, if my job is to declare a future that other people will commit to, then I have to have connection. I have to be able to truly ask for their help and enable them to come help me. When someone asks you for help—regardless of whether the person is below, above, across; your spouse; your boss; or your direct report—would you think less of them? Would you consider that weak? No, just the opposite. No one has to be a superhero. So overcome any misconceptions about asking for help and allow yourself to be vulnerable.

How do you practice asking for help? Be realistic and honest about what you know and what you don't know, and be really clear about that. Where are you not sure? For what problems could someone add insight? Then go to someone and say, "I really could use your help on this," and see what happens.

As a leader, asking for help is one of the most empowering things you can do for your team. The best bosses are the ones who are courageous enough to say, "I'm not sure how to get there. Can you help me?" Because if I can't admit that I don't know the answer to everything, then there's no room for anybody else to step up. So think about one of your current challenges, the one you really don't know how to solve. Then find one person in your stakeholder universe, and ask them to help you. Pay very close attention to the impact on the challenge, and more importantly to the relationship between the two of you. That is how you begin to ask for help.

3

Learn to Work within Fear

Most of the issues people have in leadership, working on teams, in interpersonal relationships, and within their organizations are fear based. We're afraid of losing our job or losing our edge. We're afraid of offending people. We're afraid of rocking the boat. And we fear that if we speak up, things will only get worse.

I work with leaders who declare incredibly small futures compared to what's possible because they're afraid that if they went for what they really wanted, they would fail. So they hold themselves and the entire team back. I work with some leaders who constantly avoid the necessary conversations because they're afraid people won't like them and they'll lose the harmony and consensus of the team. Meanwhile, everybody is going crazy, because they see that the decision is not getting made or the same person is poisoning the team. I see people who are afraid of giving the boss feedback that could be incredibly valuable because they're afraid of what the boss might think of them. They're afraid of being offensive. They're afraid that it's not their place. Oftentimes, the biggest fear is that the situation will get worse than it is right now. Fear is a huge impediment because it prevents leaders from taking bigger action and becoming better. It also keeps people from having the conversations they need to have.

WHY ARE WE SO AFRAID?

Fear is an emotion rooted in the potential loss of something. If we consider how emotions work, sadness occurs when we actually lose something. For example, I feel sad because I've lost an opportunity or a potential promotion at work. Fear shows up when there's a possibility of loss. We feel fear when we're afraid to lose something. Emotions are triggered by external events. An emotion is a predisposition to act, meaning that in the emotion of fear, I'm going to act in a certain way, which is very different than the way I will act in the emotion of ambition, for example. So let's say I'm walking along a dark alley at night, and I hear somebody behind me. That external event triggers the emotion of fear, which makes my heart beat faster, my muscles get tense, my eyes open up, and, based on these factors, I am predisposed to run or fight. Emotions are short lived because if I turn around in fear and see that it's my friend walking up behind me, I'm not afraid any more. It's gone. Moods, on the other hand, last longer, and they're not triggered by external events. Now what's really interesting is that when people exist in fear frequently, they can shift into what we call a mood of fear, which means they actually live in a world of fear. Everything seems dangerous and risky, but those feelings are often completely irrational.

What's so amazing about fear is that we often have heard these stories in childhood or at some point in life that warned us not to take risks and illustrated the consequences of doing so. But those stories and the fears we hold because of them don't hold up to life right now. So why let fear stop you from being your true self? No emotion biologically is good or bad. They just are. Feeling fear is perfectly normal and healthy. Success or failure, however, depends on what you do with that fear.

When it comes to leadership, fear can bring everything to a halt. Leading is declaring a future that other people will commit to, which means you actually have to inspire people to follow you. It's like horseback riding—if you're afraid, the horse knows. People know if you're afraid as a leader. This isn't to say a leader can't or doesn't feel fear. Fear isn't bad. A great leader will take action within fear, and you need to engage with other human beings, even when you are afraid.

MISSING CONVERSATIONS

Fear shows up, in many environments, with avoidance. We avoid uncomfortable situations and conversations, even when we know we shouldn't. When you really think about it, there's nothing more important to business than conversation. Whether you work for a company that sells insurance or sporting goods or social networking, conversations are what you do. If an alien came down from outer space, with no contextual knowledge of your job, what would that alien see? You're sending e-mails, you're talking to your team, you're meeting with people—all these are conversations. Basically, everything at work is a direct relation to conversations that you're having, not having, having well, or not having well. They are the key to your whole success. And yet, we spend a lot of time avoiding conversations that make us uncomfortable or feel difficult. When we have to confront a team member or bring up an issue with our boss, oftentimes we'd rather not say anything at all than speak up.

When I ask my clients what conversation they're avoiding, I'll hear things like: "I'm afraid they won't listen." "I'm afraid of exposing myself. Like I'll open myself up, and they'll use that against me." And, "What I'm most afraid of is that even though it's horrible right now, doing something might open a can of worms and make everything worse." Before spending time with teams as a group, I interview the individual team members confidentially to gain perspective on their world views and interpretations regarding what is working and what isn't. Many times everyone is looking at the same elephant in the room and not saying a word about it. When I ask why these issues aren't being brought up at team meetings, I often hear two reasons. First, we never make the time or the space to talk about this stuff because we are too busy reporting on what we are all working on. And second, no one wants to be the bad guy and bring this up because we're not sure what the leader and everyone else on the team will say.

I recently worked with a leader and his team so they could improve their team efficiency. We spent a good amount of time working on the emotions and moods on the team. Through listening, sharing stories, and paying attention to their own current emotions, the team began to see more choices, more ability to select the emotion most supportive to their next conversation. So when they felt fear and wanted to avoid a conversation, they recognized it and, as a result, could choose to have that conversation anyway. What I noticed as I helped them was that the same conversation they had attempted some time ago now went much smoother and created a very different outcome simply because they entered into the conversation, not from frustration and fear, but from curiosity and empathy. They had the ability to see the mood and then, through awareness, choose a different mood.

FACING YOUR FEARS

Courage comes from the Latin word *cor*, which means heart. When you're courageous, you're being who you are fully. Great leaders accept fear. They notice it. And they find courage to act in the fear, with the fear. Environment has so much to do with acting in the face of fear. If you've ever watched a mother with a child who is afraid of some new challenge or situation, she'll encourage the child to try the scary thing, to take the first step. And the mother lets the child know it will be okay, that she has his back. As a leader, your actions create the environment on your team. When you are honest and act in the face of fear, it encourages your team to do the same. When you allow yourself to be vulnerable, you help foster trust. This can change the team environment because everyone learns to support each other and to acknowledge and applaud each other's ability to enter into uncertainty by trying something with no guarantees, or launching a new offer, or acting in a different and uncomfortable way.

How do you become more courageous? Shift the observer—in other words, move from the dance floor to the balcony. More than half the battle with fear is noticing that you're afraid. For most people, they don't even notice. They just act in fear. They make decisions in fear; they interact with others based on fear, without ever realizing what's controlling them. Again, awareness brings choice. If I see that I'm afraid, I now have a choice. And that's really powerful.

The first step is noticing situations where you feel fear. Where are you afraid? Where are you holding back? What exactly are you afraid to lose? And is it truly at risk? Are you afraid to tell your boss the truth? Do you avoid correcting your team members? Whatever makes you feel like running the other way, notice it.

Once you practice noticing situations that scare you, you get better at finding them. So the next challenge is finding a situation that you want to avoid and, instead of walking away or avoiding it, walk in. If you are the CEO, you don't have to begin with your supervisory board—start small and practice to work up to the bigger conversations. Think of something small, and then go have that conversation. Be true to yourself despite your fear, and practice it until courage feels a bit more comfortable and familiar.

Acting despite your fear is essential to effective leadership. Consider the greater purpose of taking action within your fears. Why would you like to have that conversation? If you can't work with someone, or if the day-to-day situation would get easier, or you go home miserable every day because of what happened at the office, then isn't alleviating that feeling worth the risk? Think of how great it will feel to get rid of everything you've avoided confronting—all the conversations you're not having, all the places your pride is being hurt or your productivity hindered. Not only will you become a more effective, successful leader but your life will also be more satisfying.

4

Learn to Build and Rebuild Trust

If I were to walk in to the room and start talking about human connection, trust, and vulnerability with most leaders and teams, it would be weird. Leaders are rational and cerebral—talking about emotions makes us uncomfortable. But we can't talk about leadership without talking about this stuff because we're all human beings with emotions, and we need to lead other human beings who also have emotions.

Most of the conversations we have at work are practical and transactional—we need a piece of information for a project or we're following up. Even when we're hanging around the water cooler, we're not having conversations that really build trust and human connection. I did a two-day workshop with a senior team, and as I was interviewing them, I could see that they wanted and needed more connection and trust among the group. We spent a whole day provoking and bringing up missing conversations. And then in the evening, after a walk around the winery where the retreat was held, and a nice dinner with some wine, I said, "Let's get to know each other better." I used an exercise that asks people to identify and share a transformational moment in their lives—something that made them who they are today, but that most people didn't know about. I explained that one by one, everyone would stand up and share his or her story, and I encouraged them by saying, "You know, if you want to say your transformational moment was the first day that you joined the company, and that's all you're going to say, that's fine. Or you can bring it. You can really consider this to be a safe space and share your story. If you want to get to know each other, this is your chance."

Everyone in the room kind of shrugged and looked around. Then, one by one, they stood up and shared their deep, personal stories. There was real sharing; there were breakthroughs. It was all very human and emotional. And these were senior business-people, many of whom had known each other for years and had never had conversations like this. At the end, everyone pretty much agreed that they now saw their coworkers as real people, which they hadn't really thought about before. I know that sounds simple, and yet it's amazing to me how many teams don't know each other, don't trust each other, and don't really connect.

TRUST

Being a leader means making bigger promises about what you can deliver, because as leaders we have more resources to help us produce greater and more valuable results. And yet if we can't fully trust our people, then all we have are bigger promises and more people to manage, because we can't fully take advantage of the resources we have. It is like having a race car when you don't know how to drive.

Trust is essential because, well, consider how difficult life can be without it. Lack of trust is a key reason so many leaders end up being super performers and having such a hard time delegating. We don't know how to build and rebuild trust with others, and we are not ready to put our reputation, our promises, and our results in the hands of others. So we may give parts of the project to the team, but in reality we still control it and end up dedicating evenings, weekends, and tremendous energy worrying about the enormity of it all—or, worse, doing the work ourselves. Clients and customers take their business elsewhere when they don't feel they can trust a company. Marriages dissolve when trust is broken and can't be repaired. Without trust, success will be limited in any relationship. And so I often say to teams and leaders, if you don't have trust, I don't know where else we can start.

Charles Feltman, author of *The Thin Book of Trust: An Essential Primer for Building Trust at Work*, defines trust as, "choosing to risk making something you value vulnerable to another person's actions." And trust is an assessment. It doesn't exist somewhere out in the world; it's your own assessment of whether or not another person will fulfill their promises. Trust also exists by domain. In other words, I can trust my coworker to finish a project, but I can't trust him to fly the airplane when I go to LA. This is an exaggerated example, but people often make statements about trustworthiness, like, "Oh, Beth can't be trusted," that don't make sense. You can trust her for some things, but probably not for others. Being able to distinguish the domains where a person can and cannot be trusted is important. And if you don't trust someone, you get to take ownership of that assessment.

When I work with a team, almost every time my work starts with anonymous, confidential interviews. I do this for two reasons. First, if I'm spending two days with a team of people and working very closely with the team leader, I have to build trust with them. But the interviews also allow me to gather information about the leader and what's happening on the team. They'll tell me, oftentimes, really important missing pieces. The answer may not be straightforward, but it often boils down to a lack of trust. They'll say things like, "I don't wanna be the bad guy," or, "I could end up getting burned if I'm the one who brings this up," which suggests they don't trust their teammates not to turn on them.

So what does trust look like? When I work with a leader and her team, I have to build trust so that the leader will allow me to lead many conversations during the two days. The leader has to risk making something she cares a lot about—her team—vulnerable to my actions. I could take the front of the room and say anything, and so the leader has to trust that I know what I'm doing and will do good work. And even though she doesn't know what I'll say, that's okay. This happens because I fulfill the promises I made from the start. Trust has to be built.

What gets in the way of building trust? Why is this so hard for us? We are not taught how to do this, and we often don't feel safe opening up at work. We don't think being open and vulnerable is a positive way to be, especially not in a business environment. But I've found that people respect others for showing their vulnerability. It can take work, but when you create that safe space, human beings actually show up. The missing conversations—the issues no one wants to talk about—start happening, and the guys start talking to each other instead of about each other. What's amazing about missing conversations is that they're missing because of a lack of trust. Nobody wants to talk to someone they don't trust.

For example, I was working with a team where the holding company was based in Latam, and they owned a company in the United States. I walked into a situation where the leader of this extended team was from Colombia. And he had people in Colombia who didn't get along well with each other, and he had a bunch of people who could not speak to each other between Colombia and the United States. No one could talk to anyone about anything. Nobody wanted to speak up. And everyone was miserable because of it. There was so much mistrust that they hated each other, and the business was suffering as a result. Rebuilding trust among the team was the only place to start.

I was working with a colleague from Colombia, and after doing lots of interviews and realizing how drastic this situation was, we created a cool exercise for building trust and having the missing conversations. The meeting was held on neutral ground at an off-site hotel, and there were about fifteen people from two different countries, two different teams, with all sorts of conflicts. We created a very safe environment and the right mood and invited them to begin having missing conversation after missing conversation. That's how they spent the afternoon. And honestly, about 85 percent of their problems moved forward toward resolution. It wasn't all completely resolved, and some issues would take longer. But at least they could now get to work. During the debriefing, I heard a huge sense of relief from the team. They realized they were spending huge amounts of energy worrying about and not having these conversations, and although there was still work to do, just opening the conversation and dispelling their initial assumptions allowed them to continue in a very different emotional state.

HOW TO BUILD TRUST

To be a great leader, you need to get good at building trust, which means practice. So how can you become a more trustworthy person? Trust is like a table with four legs: sincerity, reliability, competence, and care. To build trust with others and to assess another person's trustworthiness, consider these four factors.

Sincerity means what's being said publicly is the same as what's being thought privately—in other words, telling the truth, being impeccable with your word, and saying what you mean for real. If you compliment someone and then laugh, and that person feels you're being insincere, that creates distrust. So to build trust, be honest. Be impeccable with your word.

Reliability means track record. The last five times you've told me you would handle something, did you? Mistrust starts to show up in reliability when people have to wonder if you'll do what you say you're going to do, like showing up, being on time, or following through. When people are reliable, you don't have to wonder, "Is he going to be there?" You trust that he will be.

The next one is competence. For me to be trustworthy, I need to make promises based on results and actions that I actually know how to do. So imagine you have a sixteen-year-old son who asks, "Dad, can I have the keys to the car? I'm ready." Let's say he's being sincere. He really believes he's ready, and he's quite reliable in other aspects of life, like grades and being responsible. Even when you have a great kid, if he doesn't have the driving experience and competence, you might not trust him to take the car. This doesn't mean you don't trust your kid; but for this specific request, you don't think he's ready. If you don't have competence, people may not trust you with some domains. But building your competence is the easiest of the four factors to work on.

And then the fourth factor in trust is care. If the person is sincere, and he's reliable, and he's competent, but he doesn't really care about the relationship with me and taking care of what I need, then full trust won't exist. The human element of care must exist for people to totally put their hands in the fire and trust someone.

Sincerity, reliability, competence, and care create trust, and working on whatever is lacking in those four will improve trust. However, this is not a magic pill that will solve all your problems. There are unwinnable games. Let's face it: there are some jerks out there. Some people don't care. But in my experience, so many times, when trust doesn't exist or has been broken, there's been no attempt to rebuild it because of blindness. They didn't know how to or even that they needed to. And, by the way, building trust is hard, but rebuilding it is much harder. If we don't trust each other because we've never even tried, that's hard. That takes some work. If we don't trust each other because you broke my trust, we can overcome that, but it's really hard. Knowing how to build trust can't fix everything, but being conscious of it and getting better at it is an important arrow in every leader's quiver. When you learn to recognize the four factors, you can go out and build trust where you can and let go where you can't.

Think of a real scenario where you don't trust someone right now. For most people, that's pretty easy. And if you understand the four legs of trust, then it's probably pretty easy to see why you don't trust that person. The challenge is getting the courage to actually have the conversation that will build trust. Pick the first of the missing conversations and start there.

VULNERABILITY

Who knows where we all got the idea that being a great leader means being invincible and never showing weakness. It's like everyone believes leaders are supposed to be these all powerful, nonemotional, never-flinching, answer-for-everything perfect people. And yet, it's completely counterintuitive. Brené Brown, author of *Braving the Wilderness*, says vulnerability is the ability to truly be who you are, which is important because that's when connection happens. Without making ourselves vulnerable, we can't have those missing conversations that build or rebuild trust.

Let's say your boss was vulnerable enough to say she is completely committed to owning the process and to getting us from point A to point B, but she has absolutely no idea how to do it and really needs your help. Would you lose respect for her? Almost every time I ask that question, someone looks at me and says, "You know, one time that happened to me, and that was my best boss ever." The whole point is creating a human connection, and moments like this spark totally different relationships. In business we talk all the time about accountability and ownership, and everybody says that's so important. You don't build ownership and accountability in other people by telling them what to do over and over again. You build it through that trusted relationship and through being vulnerable enough to say, "I don't have the answers. That's why I need you."

Vulnerability doesn't equal tears; you don't have to cry at work to show up as vulnerable. Vulnerability is having the courage to be who you are instead of who you think people want you to be. It comes down to authenticity, which is the birthplace of sincerity and where trust is built.

Even though no one likes talking about it, the human element of leadership and business can't be ignored or dismissed. And no team can fully trust each other or reap the benefits high trust can bring without opening up, allowing themselves to be vulnerable, and having those missing conversations. By understanding that we're all humans with emotions and practicing building trust, leaders and teams can work cohesively, increase accountability, and achieve greater success.

5

Learn to Listen

Leaders lead other human beings. If you lead machines, we can all go home. As simple as it sounds, this is something many leaders tend to forget. And leading human beings well means connecting with those people, having empathy, and listening to them.

The old command-and-control model basically says that the leader not only knows where we're going but knows the way to get there and tells everybody what to do. People get assignments and check in with their progress. But this creates a lot of back-and-forth, and the whole responsibility sits on the leader's shoulders. I often ask teams to raise their hands if they feel like they chase other people for a living. Everyone laughs when they all raise their hands, and then they sigh with dread. So leaders are totally exhausted, and the people who work for them feel disempowered.

The team members don't feel like they own anything because basically they don't, and they don't feel like anyone listens to them. In some ways, it's a very comfortable position for the follower because you just get your task and you go to work. The frustrating part is when you don't actually see the greater purpose of what you're working on, and then the rules change; you end up creating a lot of waste. And after a while, most really good people get bored because they're not bringing any creativity or any ownership into their work. But when they go in and make a suggestion, the boss is operating in a command-and-control mind-set and thinking, "What's the fastest way to get this thing done?" The leader isn't really listening.

But the leader's job is not to tell anybody how or what to do. The effective leader's job is to describe what the winnable game looks like and then engage people in all their creativity and talent to get it done. When leadership starts listening, the team members realize they own a piece of the work, and they start to create ideas.

There's a television show in the United States called *Inside the Actors Studio* that does in-depth interviews with actors. It's been on for years, and every time the host James Lipton asks, "What's really the most important part of great acting?" Most of the greats—the Streeps, and the De Niros, and the Redfords—when I watched the interview, always had similar answers. They all said something like, "It's all based on good homework. Get my character, learn my lines, and then show up and be incredibly present and listen." When they're in the scene, they have to listen to what's happening with the other people, because that's where, as the actors would say, the magic happens. It's all about listening. And it's not that much different in leadership.

If you think about any great leader you've worked for, he or she was probably great at listening to what's going on. Everyone remembers great leaders because they listened. I've met Bill Clinton a number of times, and he's renowned for this. He's like a vortex. When you talk to him, it's like there's nothing else in the world that exists in that moment for him except me. And it was real, but my guess is he had to practice. We were all taught in school to get the answer right, and none of us got great grades for asking questions. So we can't expect to be good at this. But when you see great leadership in action, the leader is present.

As a leader, you won't succeed until you get all the juice, all the great talent, out of everybody in the organization. So the key to your success is your ability to listen to where they are, what's keeping them from greatness, their concerns, and their needs. And yet when I watch most leaders, they're running a thousand miles an hour, stuck in tasks, often missing what's actually happening around them. There's so little listening actually happening, and the leaders aren't even aware of it. But everyone on the team is.

When I first learned about listening, I was the VP of sales in my corporate job. And it was a time in my life when I was traveling so much that I was home for just forty-eight to seventy-two hours and then be back on the road again. I would come home with all this energy and be so excited to see my kids, who were still little at the time, that I'd start interviewing them. "Hey, Daniel, how's it going? How's school? What's going on, man?" And my wife would pull me aside and say, "Calm down. You're coming in like a tornado and totally disrupting the house." So I had learned about listening in a workshop with my team, and the next time I came home, I tried an experiment. My youngest, who was four or five at the time, was in the bath. So I sat down in the bathroom, and instead of asking him questions, I sat there, not thinking about work or checking my Blackberry (that's what we all had back then), and I never said a word. And after a few long minutes of silence, my five-year-old started to speak. I didn't interrupt him; I just listened. And it was the first time in a long time that he talked to me like that. The lessons I learned about listening from that come to work with me every day. And for everyone, especially leaders, listening is a huge part of success. It's as essential to leadership as keeping your eye on the ball in sports.

Empathy means I'm putting myself in your shoes, but I don't necessarily have to agree with you. It doesn't mean you're right.

It means I'm willing to see the world the way you're seeing it. Listening and having conversations help create empathy, so conflicting sides can shift out of attack mode and see the situation from another perspective. Some leaders are naturally good at empathizing with others; others need more practice.

When I'm working with a client and they start complaining about what's happening with someone else's behavior, I'll ask, "Why is this person bringing that behavior? What is it they need and are not getting from you?" This completely shuts down the client's complaining because they start to see the other side of the situation. This is how you create empathy. You ask, "What's happening in their world?" And what's amazing is that most of the time, it's not that people are idiots and jerks who hate you. It's just that they're trying to take care of what matters to them, and they're seeing the world they see. As a leader, if I can get more and more practiced at seeing the world the way someone else sees it, I have a much better chance at a productive conversation rather than a fight.

When leaders are willing to take a deep breath and not automatically go into their normal reaction mode, which is either fight or flight or freeze, and consider what might be happening for this other person, most of the time it's not that hard to get to a place where you both want to end up. Great leaders create that new space to find out what's happening and to get to the solution.

Mister Miyagi from the classic 1980s movie *Karate Kid* is the perfect example. When he was teaching Daniel to wax on, wax off, and paint the fence, he wasn't telling Daniel, "Here are the five moves. Do it like I do it. Copy me." He was bringing Daniel along and allowing him to actually step up, learn, get there. Was Miyagi listening to Daniel? That's all he did. He watched; he listened. And when I watch most leaders in organizations, that's not what I see.

I see speeches. I see a lot of one-way delivery that's not even a conversation. But it's just a monologue; team leaders stand up in front of the team, and they just talk. There's no dialogue, there's no conversation, there's no listening. So let's change that.

HOW TO BE A BETTER LISTENER

In general, we're all bad at listening. I observe conversations for a living, and there's always room for improvement. When someone else is talking, we're typically thinking of the next brilliant thing we're going to say. So someone starts to speak, and I immediately—and I mean in seconds—already believe that I know where he or she is going with this, and I'm ready to give him or her the solution. The trouble is that because I wasn't listening, my solutions are often to problems they didn't even have. This won't help the person or solve problems, but because I'm the boss, no one will say anything. Listening means turning off the tendency to offer solutions.

Often people aren't really asking for advice in the first place. They're just venting or beginning, in their own mind, to understand what's actually wrong. But because a listener jumps so quickly to solution mode, we never get there, which causes more frustration later for both parties. Instead, a better approach is learning to pause, to ask open-ended questions, and to actually listen to what's being said and what's not being said. By doing this, we can help the people in front of us explore and find their own answer, as opposed to handing them something that may or may not be of use. When really good listening happens, it gives the people bringing the issue the chance to not only express their initial thought, but potentially get closer to the real issue.

Most people I work with aren't doing anything to practice their listening skills. They're doing "their job." But if you've been promoted into a management or leadership position or if you are C-suite in an organization with thousands of people, your most important job is listening to your people and getting the very best production and performance out of them. Again, when we allow ourselves to get caught up in the task, doing what we know instead of truly leading, overwhelm starts to show up. So if one of the key fundamental skills to leadership is listening and human connection, then what are you as a leader doing on an ongoing basis to build that muscle? What are you doing to get better?

When I'm working with leaders and teams, I have a listening exercise where they sit in pairs. One of them talks for a couple of minutes about a real challenge or issue they have at work, while the other person practices just listening. They don't interrupt or say anything, and they listen. What's happening is I'm giving both people the chance to listen and be listened to without interruption, which is vastly different than our normal life. When I ask people to do this exercise, many tell me they struggle with not interrupting. And even though it feels amazing not to be interrupted, the person being listened to is usually uncomfortable because we're all so used to interruptions. This is an artificial exercise, like when you're doing piano scales; it's exaggerated for the sake of the learning. In real life, you probably won't be letting someone talk for two minutes without saying anything at all. But practicing this in my own life has made me more effective at work and even at home. Not telling my wife immediately what my solution is has had a great effect on us, and it's not hard to see why.

Asking questions, instead of giving advice, is an essential element of good listening. Leaders often ask me how to stop giving advice in these situations, and, in my experience, it's been an act of humility. Who the hell do I think I am, thinking that I know better than you do? When someone comes to you with an issue, it's his life, his job, his work—he's in the middle of it, so how could I know better? A leader's job is not to believe that she knows more than the other person, even if she is the boss. The leader's job is to help the other person figure it out. So we listen, and maybe we'll paraphrase. And oftentimes when someone hears what the other person heard, they get closer to what's really going on.

When someone comes to me and says, "I'm not sure about something," that person may initially be looking for an answer. But if you say, "Okay, so tell me what concerns you, and what are some ideas you have about that?" you show that you truly want the person to succeed and you're giving her space. That's really important in listening. You're giving people enough space and trusting that they probably have a better answer than you will. It's incredibly exciting and empowering. And this is how you create more empowerment and more accountability in your organization. This is how it works.

Another listening skill to practice is called congruence. Congruence means my emotional state and my body are aligned with what I'm saying. One of the best ways to understand congruence is to experience incongruence. If you stand up and stretch your arms up to the sky and smile and try to say, "I'm so depressed," it won't sound or feel genuine. So listening sometimes includes watching for incongruence. If you're really listening to someone, and they say, "I'm doing great," but their body language tells a different story, then you can say to the person, "It doesn't look like that." Now, this doesn't mean you're right or wrong; you're just making an observation. And that can help the other person potentially go to a different place and share more.

Part of trust is building a safer space, being sincere, and showing that you actually do care about the people on your team. When I see great leaders, that's what they're doing. They're creating lots of space for people to share what's really going on and where they're stuck. They're allowing room for mistakes. Mistakes are how innovation and transformation happen, but people still get snubbed for making them. If you're going to build a culture where it's okay to innovate and it's okay to make mistakes, you need to be able to listen to what your people are ready for, what are they afraid of, and what they need to step up and take more risks.

LISTENING BETTER IN THE FUTURE

Listening means getting up on the balcony to see what's happening. Nelson Mandela, Mahatma Gandhi, and all the great leaders of our time were good at listening. So how are you at it? What's your practice? What are you going to do to get better? You don't have to be a master to see results. And one of the greatest side benefits of my work is when I get e-mails from spouses saying, "I know you're working with my wife or my husband on their business, but I just want to say thank you. It's made a huge difference at home too." The moment anyone starts practicing something like listening with their direct reports, it spreads to other conversations and relationships. And guess what? Life gets so much better.

6

Learn to Manage Outcomes, Not Tasks

If you're the boss, your job is to manage your own promises and make sure the people who work for you are managing theirs. That's very different from knowing how to do everything and telling everyone on your team how to do their work. Because most of us were raised in command-and-control leadership models, the way we learned, the way our bosses led us, is we tell people what to do, we tell them how to do it, and then we tell them what's wrong with it when they're done. And then we chase people. We send e-mails asking, "How's it going? When can I expect to get what I asked for? What's happening with the project?" For the leader, this is exhausting. And it's not empowering for the direct report. Telling people what to do and how to do it doesn't foster buy-in and eventually leads to disengaged team members.

The better way is what *Harvard Business Review* calls promise-based management. A promise is a specific measurable outcome by a certain date. If you think about it, promises are how organizations get work done—we're all requesting things from other people and delivering on requests others have asked from us. And when the leader manages promises instead of micromanaging and chasing after tasks, everything shifts. People start owning their work, finding solutions, and communicating better with each other. If you want to create accountability in your organization, this is how it's done.

THE CYCLE OF THE PROMISE

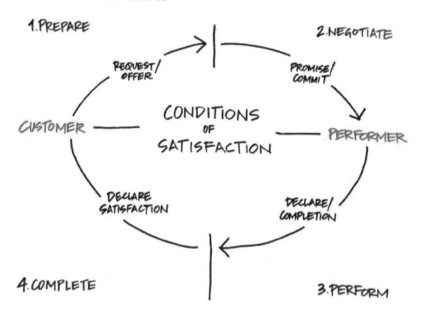

Promise-based management means being aware of the cycle of the promise and using it to eliminate the frustration that's often involved with needing something from someone else. Instead of thinking in terms of the boss and the direct report, the cycle of the promise has a customer and a performer for an outcome that will satisfy the customer. The customer could be anyone because that person is the customer of the promise. The customer has to be clear on the terms of his or her satisfaction, and when the cycle starts during the request or offer, the customer has to communicate those terms of satisfaction to the performer. The performer then makes the promise—the specific measurable outcome with a delivery date. Then the performer performs the request and declares completion when it's finished. Finally, the customer declares satisfaction.

So instead of command-and-control leadership, where you tell your direct report, "I want you to do it like this, and I want a report that looks like this," you, as the customer, explain what you need and why. And then you ask, "What can I count on from you?" This is an effective request. Then the performer needs to actually respond to this request with a specific and measurable outcome with a delivery date. So, for example, the performer might respond by committing to having the agreed upon report in my inbox every second Friday. And then on the next second Friday, your team member sends the report and declares completion, and you, as a good customer, write back and say, "Thanks. It looks great." That's a perfectly executed cycle of the promise. And understanding this cycle can improve the way your organization works and reveal reasons why work isn't getting done.

But the huge shift comes when we move into a world where you're not delegating like handing out playing cards, "Go do this, go do that, go do this." This type of leadership encourages distrust and disengagement, and it doesn't allow your team to take ownership over their work. In promise-based management, you're saying, "This is what I need the world to look like." And then asking your people, "What can I count on from you?" That's such an amazing question.

Now, what happens most of the time is the leader says to the direct report, probably in a meeting where a thousand different things are being discussed, "Hey, that report that I'm going to need every second Friday, we're good, right?" And the direct report, who may or may not know what the leader is talking about, says, "Yeah, yeah, okay," because there's no time to talk about it, and he or she doesn't want to say no to the boss. In this example, the request wasn't clear, and neither were the conditions of satisfaction. Most importantly, the promise was never actually made by the performer. Breakdowns happen because pieces of the cycle are missing.

Even the declaring completion and declaring satisfaction pieces are essential. If you don't declare completion, then, as a performer, you let your customer down because they have to come looking for you. How many times have you declared completion on something and gotten silence in return? Maybe your customer didn't see the e-mail or got busy and forgot, and the performer is left wondering. In the absence of data, we make stuff up. We start to think, "Oh, it must be that he didn't like the report or he didn't care or he didn't really need it." Then the next time this person asks you to do something, you're a lot more hesitant. And all you needed was just, "Hey, great. Thanks, got it."

The cycle of the promise is not some nifty thing that I was taught. This exists. It's nondiscretionary. It's real. It's happening. We live this all day long. The only question is, do you see it or not? And awareness brings choice.

We can really see the power of the cycle of the promise when we apply it to different situations. So let's say, as the customer, to be satisfied I need to receive a report every week that explains the status of a project. I could go to my direct report and tell him, "I want you to work on this report, and this is what it should look like, and I want it to be on Excel, and I want it by Friday," and give all the details. In this case, I'm the customer, and I've given the performer what I need to be satisfied. But I haven't left room for any response but "Yes sir." There's no way for the performer to add input or suggest a better way to do it. There's no way to have a conversation. And the performer either goes back to his desk and works on it or doesn't.

In this case, not only was I unclear on the purpose of my request but also I never really got a promise. The person nodded, or I got an e-mail back that said, "Yep, I'm on it. I'll see what I can do." This wasn't a specific measurable outcome by a certain date. When you don't have that, you don't have a promise. And when you don't have a promise, things very often don't get done. Progress stalls. Accountability goes missing. So much of all the crap that exists in organizations starts right here in these little missing links.

MANAGING PROMISES

I had a client who was in charge of a sales team, and when I met with him, he told me he was frustrated because sales numbers were down and he couldn't seem to get his team to do anything about it. He said, "I just keep telling the team we're falling short of the $ million-dollar company goal, and they've got to get out and make more phone calls. I tell them, 'This is serious, guys. We're behind, and you've got to get your ass in gear and start selling more.' And I don't understand why they don't actually react to this. I mean they hear me, but I don't see anything changing."

Applying the cycle of the promise to this situation, I asked him, "Do you have the promise? Who's promising this?" He needed to realize he was the only one owning the sales number. Later I was talking to one of his team members and asked, "What do you do?"

He said, "I'm working really hard, trying to get the number for him. I'm trying to, you know, sell more or whatever."

I said, "Okay, but what's your promise?"

"$ million-dollars."

"No, no, no, $ million-dollars is the company's promise. That's the total number for the organization. What's your promise?"

"Oh, I don't know. It's just to do as much as I can."

Well, that's the problem. So with this particular leader, I invited a totally different conversation. Instead of telling the team they need to do more, the leader has to make each team member understand that his or her job depends on satisfying the leader's needs, because the leader owns the team's shared promise. The leader has to help the team build and commit to the shared promise and understand why it's important, and then the leader has to ask each team member, "What can you do to help us get there?" The leader then helps each team member achieve the promised outcome. That's how this works. If your team member missed his or her outcome, that team member has to come up with a recovery plan; it's his or her promise. The leader is there to help, but the promise belongs to the person who made it. For most leaders and teams, this is an entirely new way to look at work. And it changes everything.

A promise is when someone says in her own words what she's going to produce, and what she's going to produce is not, "The best I can." It's an actual measurable thing by a specified date. If you don't have that, you don't have anything; that's your problem. So if you want to be a satisfied customer, you need to get better at explaining the conditions of your satisfaction and helping people learn to make promises.

As the customer, you have to be clear about your conditions of satisfaction, and you have to get a promise from the performer. That's the key, because you, as the leader, don't delegate the task. You don't determine how the promise is fulfilled. You let the team members invent the solution. And when the promise is delivered, you make sure you're satisfied. If not, then you have a conversation with the performer about how to get there.

I notice a tremendous amount of gossip, and what I call "victim energy" in organizations. People sit around, complaining about what's wrong, and what I learned years ago is that a complaint is only valid when a promise has not been fulfilled. If you notice yourself complaining, or if you notice someone on your team complaining, a really powerful generative leadership move is to ask yourself or the person, "What promise has been made that has not been fulfilled?" And most of the time, there was never a promise made. There was never even a request. We live in a world where we assume that what we think is the way it should be. And if that's not the case, we complain. Making this distinction with complaints changes everything because instead of going into victim mode, you take action. You actually move from defense into offense by making a powerful request and getting a promise. Using the cycle of the promise can alleviate the victim energy and keep everything moving forward.

When I implemented the cycle of the promise with my team, I had to actually sit down with them and say, "I'm sick of micromanaging you, I'm sick of staying late on Friday nights, and I'm sure you're sick of just doing it my way. So I'm no longer going to tell you how to do things. I'm committing to telling you what the end game looks like. And I'm going to ask you to make a promise to tell me what you're going to give me by when." For a leader who doesn't like conflict, it can be difficult to hold people accountable and ask questions like, "What can I count on from you?" But you're actually saying to your team: "You invent it." And slowly people step up. I often found that my team would get there a totally different way than I had ever imagined. But as long as the goal is met, who cares how they get there? I realized that my job was not to spend Friday nights doing presentations that my team didn't quite understand. My job was to let them do everything the way they do it, in their style, and help them deliver the promises they've given me. Help manage crisis situations, help them when they're not in a good space, be their coach, be their mentor—that's what a leader should be doing.

MAKE BETTER OFFERS

The ability to make strong offers is the flip side of making strong requests, and it means switching from offense to defense. I work a lot with service functions, like legal, HR, IT, and all these departments that provide services to the business. They often get stuck because the business is not making efficient requests of their time. They're asking them to do stuff, but it's not the right way to ask, and so they end up complaining and in victim mode because they're so upset by how inefficient everything is. One of the reasons they're stuck is they don't know how to make offers.

Making offers means learning how to listen more to what the business actually needs. These departments play offense by going in front of the business and saying, "We see you're trying to achieve this, and here's how we can help." All of a sudden, legal or IT or HR is in a business conversation, not a service-function conversation. The service function is now creating an offer. They're creating their promise, not based on what someone requested, but designing it themselves. That motivates them. And it stops the complaining about being undervalued and capable of more.

The challenge is talking about results instead of process. I worked with a top technology consulting firm years ago, and their challenge was that they wanted their technical salespeople to get better at listening and being focused on solutions, not the technical part. The guy I was working for, who was leading the team and was very frustrated, said, "It's like I'm trying to have my guys sell a Jacuzzi and talk about the feeling of the bubbles on your back and how amazing you feel. And all they want to do is talk about the scientific way that the tubes are used to heat the water." People talk way too much about what they're going to do, their plan, and how they're going to get there. And the customer doesn't care at all. All the customer wants to know is, "What will I, the customer, get at the end of all this?" That's making an offer—the business cares about results, not the process the person or function making the promise chooses to use.

USE STATUS UPDATES

A team is two or more people with a shared promise. And in many cases, the promise is so big that no one could ever fulfill it alone; we need each other. Teams have to come together as a group in meetings to make that happen—but meetings are often annoying. We prepare, and we get there and talk, and we listen to everyone else talk, and then we leave feeling like we've wasted our time. The problem is that we're having the wrong conversations. What happens, particularly in a command-and-control environment, when everyone has to say something at the meeting, they fall into talking about what they're working on: "I'm making calls, and I've got a meeting coming up that I'm preparing for, and I'm going to start working on this…" No one cares what you're working on. Maybe the boss cares, maybe the person speaking cares, but nobody else on the team cares because it doesn't apply to them. So I invite you to try never doing that again. You don't need to talk about what you're working on anymore. The only conversation you're having in every meeting all the time is, "What's the status of the promise?"

In an ideal world, all promises would be fulfilled. But we don't know what's going to happen, so promises have to be managed. Managing promises means the performer either fulfills it or immediately lets the customer know what's getting in the way. And if the promise isn't on track, the team cares. Because if one person doesn't make it, the shared promise is now in jeopardy.

There are four potential statuses for any promise. The first is "on track," and the other three are called red flags. Ideally, every promise is on track. But if you raise your hand and say, "Three of my promises are on track; one of them is off," that's an opportunity to figure out why it's off and what help you need.

The first red flag is, "something's happened, but I have a recovery plan." Things come up, and often promises depend on factors outside our control. What's important about this red flag is that as soon as something delays the promise, the performer tells the customer. In matrix organizations, where people are managing all sorts of conversations, not telling someone about a delay or problem affects the promises they've made to other customers. So you're not just letting down your customer; you're letting down their customers as well. The minute you see something happen— the minute you get that e-mail from the board about pushing back the meeting, for example—you let the customer know, and you make a recovery plan: "Hey, this is what just happened, and here's what I'm doing about it."

The second red flag is to go to your customer and ask for help. Basically, you're going back and saying, "My recovery plan is not working; let's see if we can come up with something better."

And then the third red flag is to renegotiate the promise. For example, "I just want you to know it looks like the board is not going to have this meeting. What can I do instead?"

What happens if the performer can't meet the customer's request? The cycle of the promise leaves room to negotiate and say no without actually refusing the request. If your boss says she needs your team to sell $7 million, instead of saying, "No, we can't do that," you can commit to commit. You can say something like, "I understand you want seven million dollars; let me talk to my team, and I'll be back to you in two weeks with what we can commit to."

Here you've promised to make a promise within a certain amount of time. This allows you to answer every request promptly and negotiate the promise. And it prevents you from making promises you can't keep. If you're leading a team of five people, you don't make promises to your boss without having solid promises from your team. So if your boss says, "I need seven million dollars," you go back to your team and say, "Okay, my customers are asking for seven million; what can I count on from each of you, and how can I help you?" Then we start to go. And if my people figure out they can get to $6.7 million and it feels like I can really trust it, I have a negotiation. But I'm making my own promises to my customers based on promises that I'm getting from performers, and that changes everything. In command and control, the number just gets pushed down each level, and the best we can hope for is compliance.

USING THE CYCLE OF THE PROMISE TO GENERATE A BETTER FUTURE

For almost any situation where you feel frustrated that something isn't working or isn't getting done, you can use the cycle of the promise to figure out why. Determine who the customer is, who the performer is, what the request is, and what the promise is. Then figure out what's missing.

This is another practice that can be beneficial in all areas of life. My wife and my kids have kind of grown up using the cycle of the promise, and we practice it all the time. For example, I'll send a text to my wife requesting, "Can you take care of this for me?" And she'll write me back and say, "I'm on it. I'll take care of that." And then she'll write me back six hours later and go, "It's done." And I'll write back and say, "Thank you." That sounds totally trivial, but it's actually huge because it means I don't have to chase. I don't have to remember when I come home to ask her, "What happened with this thing?" It's clean. We use it all the time, and it eliminates so much waste and creates so much more flow to be able to have conversations about more important things.

The cycle of the promise is powerful because these strategies are generative. You can understand this and make a promise or make a better request tomorrow and change the future. These practices are essential to success and satisfaction. And when you take advantage of the cycle of the promise, all of a sudden life starts to get a little easier, overwhelm starts to go away, and everything starts to work better.

7

Learn to Live Well in Uncertainty

I had a client once come to me because he was getting feedback about not seeing the bigger picture, not thinking strategically, and staying too much in the tactical day-to-day activities. When he reached out, he described feeling like he was facing one breakdown after the next. Because he didn't know how everything would turn out, he wasn't making decisions or taking action on issues that were harming the company. He kept saying to me, "But if you and I can work together, and I know that in a year from now it's going to be okay, then I see how I can do this." He was paralyzed because he felt he needed to know what the future would look like. And because he couldn't—no one can—his world was falling apart.

I see this in leaders, in human beings, all the time: this really deep need to know that everything's going to be okay. No one can guarantee what tomorrow holds. The need to know can affect everything, and oftentimes we don't even notice ourselves needing to know. When we were arranging our next meeting, I provoked that same client by saying, "I think where you're getting stuck most of the time is you need everything to be black and white and clear, and the world isn't clear. So in our next session, let's really take a look at your relationship with certainty and uncertainty." When he wrote to confirm the meeting, his message read, "I look forward to our first session on 29 June at 1300 hours. Subject: How to Deal with the Unknown." And so I wrote him back, "Me too, and that may be the subject, or not. Notice the desire to know exactly what we'll be working on." My point was that he was falling into the exact trap I meant to help him avoid, and I wanted him to recognize that. It was like in the movie *Life of Brian*, where Brian goes to the window, and there are hundreds of people waiting to hear what he's going to say. And he said, "You're all individuals." And they chanted in unison, "We are all individuals."

Here's another example of what the need to know looks like. A few years ago, I had a client who was an engineer—a profession filled with people who, by the way, tend to really love knowing and planning—who, before making decisions and taking action, he wanted everything to be planned out and needed to know it would all work out. I talked to him about how no one can predict the future, and then I said, "Do you see that it makes sense to develop a better relationship with uncertainty? Do you see that your ability to walk into that unknown is going to help you?" And we started to talk about that.

Then he said to me, for real, "Craig, if you can just help me see what it's going to look like for the next three months, this whole unknown thing, I swear I can do it."

We like everything to be laid out with high levels of certainty; knowing makes us comfortable. And yet life is messy. Not everything has a plan. It doesn't all make sense. Fighting that reality can hold us back. Leaders resist creating visions, which means they aren't doing their job. Leading—declaring a future that other people will commit to—means you, as the leader, have to enter uncharted territory without a map. You have to promise to put a man on the moon whether you know how to get there or not. If you need to know, and you're constantly attached to things being stable, you can't lead. The leader needs to be the one that takes the step and says, "This is where we're going. This is what it's going to look like. And I invite you all to jump on and create the path to get us there."

Instead, I find that I'm working with top leaders who are somehow enamored and lost in spreadsheets, formulas, and tactical conversations because they're totally avoiding their job, which is to go out into the unexplored, to create vision, and to declare where we're going. They get sucked into the smaller conversations because it's more controllable, it's known, it's comfortable, it's safe. And I see whole organizations that constantly struggle with change. Everyone says they're restructuring, that there's a reorganization, that change is happening. And underneath all that change, everyone is basically saying, "I just hope it'll all go away, and it'll go back the way it was, and things will be stable again." Has it ever really been stable? There's always hope, I suppose. But I'm trying to provoke the idea that that makes no sense. Stop resisting what is and trying to create stability that doesn't exist and never will. And rather, get really comfortable with the constant change, with the unknown, with not knowing how you're going to get there and what it's all going to look like, so you can lead.

HOW TO NOT KNOW

I often work with leaders who don't consider not knowing to be an option. And yet if we don't know, that's okay. Not having all the answers leaves room for others to bring their ideas, their creativity, their personality. When I was coached around living in uncertainty, I practiced noticing every time I needed to know. And once I started noticing, it was unbelievable how many times a day I actually wanted to know. Is this the right length of the presentation? Is it too early to send this e-mail? Is this the right e-mail to send?

If I say that, what are they going to think? Will I sell enough this year? Should I be making more efforts? Should I be calling more people? Should I just let go and not worry about it? On and on and on and on.

In addition to noticing my need to know, the second part of my practice was saying to myself, "I don't know." So every time I caught myself wanting to know, I'd smile and remind myself that I don't. The more I did it, the more I realized how little I actually knew. I mean, really, how much does anyone absolutely know about anything? And the whole thing became quite liberating, to be honest—because if I don't have to know, then the pressure's off.

Right around the time I started practicing this, I was also at the point in my career when I left corporate and started my business. And I remember a very excruciating—but also very freeing—conversation with my mother-in-law about what I was going to do for a living. She said to me, in Spanish, "What are you going to do next?"

"I don't know."

"But how are you going to support your wife and your kids?"

"I don't know." She probably wanted to kill me. But I was being completely honest, and the practice has stayed with me over the last ten years. I still get caught up in questions about the future, but I don't know. And I can't let it paralyze me; none of us can. We have work to do, visions to cast, and promises to fulfill. So one of the best things I can do for my clients is help them develop a healthier relationship with uncertainty. A lot of the fear, the discomfort, and the stuff that goes on in our life is resisting or pretending that we know, when there's no way that we can know.

Not knowing is okay. And oftentimes, when the direct report asks us for an answer, or our boss asks us for an answer, the most powerful leadership move is to be honest and say, "I don't know, and I'll find out," or, "I don't know, and where do we go from here?" But I think we get stuck feeling like our job is to either know or pretend we know. And it's simply not authentic; it's not true.

David Ogilvy was an advertising genius who said, "Half of everything we create in this agency is pure shit; I just never know which half." That's the paradox so many of my clients live in. How do you know what move to make? Well, we don't. We don't know. So what do you do? Leaders have to be able to deal with uncertainty. And when I share this when I'm with teams, everybody gets it. How do you actually build the muscle that allows you to notice uncertainty and make a move anyway?

The first step is always to really take a hard look at your own relationship with uncertainty, with the unknown. That's first and foremost. And if you realize, "Man, I really don't like it," ask yourself why not. What is it that scares you about not knowing?

Discovering your relationship to the unknown means pushing yourself with questions. When I'm working on this with clients, I'll often ask, "What is your relationship with uncertainty?" It's a very funny question, but it gets people going, and often they say they hate it. When I invite them to go a little further by asking why, the conversation usually unfolds something like this:

"Because I like to know."

"Why?"

"Because if I know, then I have a level of control and guarantee that things are going to be okay."

"Why does that matter?"

"Because I don't want to waste my time on things that don't matter." And as I continue to go deeper and deeper, what I typically find is that, at the end, what's there is a fear of failure, and a desire to know that, "I'm okay." And what's amazing to me is that I don't think we can ever feel fully okay, or satisfied, with external input. Nobody can tell you that you're okay. It comes from within.

So in many ways, by owning a healthier relationship with the unknown—having the ability to say, "I am okay not knowing"— that's when we actually realize, "I'm okay." Truly feeling satisfied and at peace—a huge part of that for me means accepting and being really okay with not knowing. Really, really okay. Like, it's incredibly liberating to write a book and have a business and not know if any of this is going to be the right answer or work or be successful. And it truly is okay. I don't know, and it's okay. Since I'm not hooked into needing to know, I don't get stuck; I just keep going. In my past, until I saw the actual road, I wouldn't take the first step. So I didn't walk very far. I didn't take any risks. I wasn't able to grow in many ways because I needed to know before I could take the step.

Practicing noticing the need to know and declaring that you don't know is essential here. Embodiment means moving away from the language and actually reaching a place where you're living it. Practicing over and over again is the only way to get it in your body.

When I learned Spanish, I took classes for years and years, and in my third year of college, I moved to Madrid and started taking the process of learning the language seriously. I had Spanish roommates, and I really wanted to understand them. And so I would go to bed at night and not allow myself to fall asleep until I could say the names of things in a given room in my apartment. One night I'd do the kitchen, and I would say the Spanish words for can opener, refrigerator, stove, and everything else I could visualize. And the next night, I'd pick a different room. It was my practice. Then I got to the point where I was really good at translating quickly. I could sit down and watch a movie on TV and listen to them speaking, and as I heard it, my brain translated it into English. At the end of a two-hour movie, I understood what had happened, but I was exhausted.

Finally, I don't remember the exact day, but after practice, and practice, and practice, and being immersed in the language, there came a point when I achieved what I call "embodiment." I stopped translating, and I started living in Spanish. I didn't have to really think about the language, and I became more connected to what I was saying. But this came with practice.

By practicing noticing the need to know and letting go of it, we can embody it and actually become okay with not knowing. Practicing until we embody whatever it is that we're practicing is essential for everything I've covered in this book. It's like learning to drive a car. At first we have to think about what our feet are doing, when to shift, and all the traffic rules. But repetition creates fluency, and when you achieve it, you can drive your car and listen to music or talk to your passenger or think about the meeting you're heading to, and you won't even remember making driving decisions. And we all know this feeling. That's embodiment.

Understanding the concept of uncertainty is not enough. We must actually notice in our own minds how often we come back to this need to know, and learn, as it happens, to notice it, and accept it, and be okay with not knowing. Give yourself permission. And as we do that over, and over, and over, we shift our relationship with uncertainty. We can develop almost like a friendship with something that used to be the enemy.

The other piece that's interesting, I think, is that we spend so much time trying to be what we think others want us to be, as opposed to just being who we are. That makes it hard as well. Part of accepting the unknown is just accepting, "I'm going to trust that

I'm doing my best and be who I am." And yet I run into a lot of people who don't even know who that actually is. So you just come back to, "What do I know right now?"

You can still take a next step, even though you don't know if you're taking the right one. You take a really deep breath. You come back to the basics of what matters. And given that, what do you think, sometimes intuitively, is the right direction? Take the next step. And then measure. Practice until you live well in uncertainty, because getting paralyzed when we don't know the answers is just wasteful.

YOUR RELATIONSHIP WITH UNCERTAINTY

In the corporate world, we're used to having a paycheck. We're used to having an order that comes with picking a plan and executing it. We make Excel spreadsheets, and we cross our Ts, and it all makes sense. That's what creates tremendous comfort. And yet it doesn't always work. I'm not saying that having structure and making plans are bad ideas. I actually think those are really important skills. I'm saying that most people I work with already have practiced structuring and planning for years. Now we have to practice something else.

If leadership is declaring a future that other people will commit to, and I realize that when I declare that future, I don't know exactly how we're going to get there, my ability to accept uncertainty is actually what allows me to lead in a mood of confidence. When I interact with leaders who are more comfortable with uncertainty, with the unknown, I find they are better at innovation, better at listening, better at being calm in crisis. And mostly, they're just much better, much more effective, in the current world. Because the world we live in is changing faster and more dramatically than it ever has before. Most of us, I'd be willing to bet, live in a world that's mostly uncertain. So our ability to be comfortable with that and surf that wave, as opposed to constantly resisting it, is often the difference between failure and success, satisfaction and dissatisfaction.

8

Learn to Build a Strong Team

The best definition of a team that I've ever learned is two or more people who have a shared promise that will produce value for the team's customer. But when I go out and work—and about 50 percent of my work is with teams—I find that even when a group of people calls themselves a team, they don't actually fit the definition. They're more what I call a workgroup.

A workgroup is two or more people who have one thing in common, normally the same boss. The reason they hold meetings is because they all report to the same person, which is why these meetings are often so boring and so irrelevant. To truly be a team, everyone involved understands that they are working toward something bigger than their own projects. They make a shared promise—a specific tangible outcome by a given date—that they want to produce together for a specific customer, typically the team leader's boss. And that promise, if it's a shared promise, is bigger than anything anyone on that team could do by themselves.

Being a team means everyone has to realize that producing results in my division or my area or my function, or whatever we call it, is the means rather than the end. In other words, what shifts is I'm no longer just in charge of doing my thing, throwing it over the fence, and then saying, "Good luck, guys; I did my part." On a team, I am there to produce results (through the work of my team and their teams) that contribute to the team's shared promise. And I have bought into that; the team's promise is my promise. This means that if someone on the team is having a breakdown or an issue, it's my problem. Because if my teammate fails, we're not going to deliver the team promise, and that's now my concern as well. So when you work on a team, a team meeting takes on a completely new importance. I'm very interested in hearing the status of the promises of my teammates because they're talking about my promise, the team promise.

Great sports teams see a shared promise, which is winning the Super Bowl, winning the Champions League, winning the World Cup, way beyond how many goals each individual player will score that year. They see their individual contributions as part of getting them to that shared promise. They're very clear about that. And yet what's fascinating is when I walk into most corporate teams and ask them, "What's your shared promise? What is that measurable end result that all of you are fully committed to producing?" I find that people are not good at answering that question. Over and over again, team leaders have been promoted into that position—as I've mentioned in other chapters—not because they were incredibly good at leading teams, but because that's the way organizations reward good performance. You get a promotion, you're now a manager, you're now a leader, and you have a team.

I saw a video of Fred Kofman, author of *Conscious Leadership*, where he used soccer to explain one of the biggest problems with teams. If the team wins the match, you get three points. If you tie the match, you get one. And if you lose, you get zero. Let's say I'm a defender and my team is losing the match one–nil. If my commitment is to the team, then that means I would abandon my defense job to go help the offense try to score. Doing so means risking that the other team will score again, but we're already losing, which means my team gets zero points. The potential reward if I go up and help my team score is that we might tie or win the match. So it actually makes sense for me to let go of my defense position and go help the offense. But it doesn't work that way in organizations, even when everyone says they want the team first.

The problem is that each team member's annual review and bonus is based on individual performance. In other words, at the end of the year, we're going to look at a very simple spreadsheet to determine how many goals were scored against us. If that number is high, you're getting less of a bonus. Your bonus, your family's ability to go to Hawaii, is totally contingent on you not letting the other team score. So while your coach might say, "Go team," you're probably going to say, "You know what? Good luck up there. I'm going to just stay here and make sure they don't score any more goals." Because that's what you're measured on.

Kofman didn't offer an answer to this conflict, and I don't have one either. But provoking the question has value. As long as bonuses and rewards are based on individual performance only, it will be hard to get people to truly commit to the team. (I often bring this challenge to my clients who work in HR and have really interesting conversations regarding how the compensation plans and reward systems might change in the future to foster more effective teams. HR functions around the world are on a path toward being seen as more strategic, and their biggest challenge will be the ability to create innovation and drive the changes necessary to shift organizational culture.)

Becoming a team means building a really strong shared promise. But this can't happen unilaterally. The team leader can't just say, "We're a team." It doesn't work like that. The team needs to commit. So there's a really important conversation where the team decides what they want to be.

Oftentimes workgroups have no idea they aren't functioning as a team. So as we go back to the awareness-brings-choice concept, I help workgroups see that they're a workgroup and see the possibility of becoming a team. And then we have a conversation about what it takes to become a team and what that change actually involves. What are the fears? What are the benefits? Because it's a huge decision. It means breaking down the silos and realizing that now my job is primarily about contributing to this team. It also means that I'm responsible, just like everybody else, for the outcome of this team. Because up until now, I'm just out doing my job—I'm the marketing person or I'm the finance person—and if I do what I say I'm going to do, I'm done. Only the team leader had to worry about the big picture. One of the big problems in organizations is no one's really owning it. And if there is someone, it's just one person. That's crazy.

By the way, deciding to remain a workgroup, which I've seen a team do before, is okay. There is no judgment. In fact, in some ways, it simplifies life a lot. If you decide that you're a workgroup, you actually don't need to meet as much. You don't need to have the conversations. That means everybody meets with the leader, and maybe you decide that quarterly you'll meet to talk about what everyone is working on and share best practices. But I don't see it happen very often.

People, when they see the choice, realize pretty quickly that there are so many benefits to becoming a team that even though it's hard, they make that decision. Most matrix organizations need cross-functional performance where people have the ability to work across divisions, across departments, across functions. Even though everyone says they live in silos, everyone is acutely aware that that's not the most effective way to do business. Working in silos creates frustration and inefficiency, and it's not fun. So when people are given the opportunity to break down the silos, become a team, practice collaboration, practice sharing, and practice helping each other, it's so much better. It makes so much more sense. If you can clarify the standards and clarify the shared promise, then people can coordinate action and call themselves a team. And that's when the fun begins in many ways.

HOW TO BECOME A TEAM

Once you've decided to become a team, how do you get there? How do you make the necessary changes?

Creating team standards is a great starting point. You can also call this laying ground rules. And I'll often go in and work with a team on verbalizing and writing down the behaviors that they value as a team and are going to commit to. Most workgroups have never had this conversation. But incredible power exists in writing down and agreeing on how we behave as a team.

When I ask teams what they value, they often answer with words like "respect" and "collaboration." But ground rules need to be more specific than that. You can't go respect someone. So I bring the question, "What would that look like?" "Respect" is a great word, but it's not generative. So we go deeper. What would it look like? What would I see you doing if you respected each other? And someone might say we don't interrupt each other in meetings. We actually listen and let one person speak at a time. I can actually observe that behavior, so it could be a ground rule. A ground rule around collaboration might be asking for help and offering to help another. Another example of respect might be punctuality. And I find over and over that one person on the team thinks that if you're not there five minutes before the meeting starts, you're late.

And another person on the team thinks that if you arrive five or ten minutes after the meeting starts, that's punctual. So what happens is the person who is early waits for ten minutes every single time, doesn't talk about this, but gets really pissed off. It creates distrust and new missing conversations because no one ever stopped to say, "How do we all agree to act as a team?"

The other amazing benefit of having team standards is that most teams are fluid. In other words, during a given year, people are constantly leaving the team and joining the team. So teams need to get really good at onboarding new members. And a great way to do that is with a very clear set of team standards that new team members get as soon as they join. Again, elite sports teams do this well. And yet we go into organizations and people are expected to come together as a team naturally, whatever that means. But it doesn't work without clear standards.

LEADING YOUR TEAM

If you're a team performer, your major responsibilities are to live the standards of the team, to be a contributing member, and to manage and report on your own promises. Every team member that I work with is, in themselves, a team leader to another team. A CEO might have nine people who report to her, but every one of those nine people is an incredibly important boss to other people in the organization. Your job as a team member is to show up, participate, and live the standards, but also manage the promises from your own area toward that shared promise.

Team leaders are often mistaken in thinking that they need to have the answers to every question and direct every aspect of the team. This is not true. Instead, the team leader needs to confirm and reconfirm, as much as possible, the conditions of satisfaction of the team's customer.

The first thing that the team leader needs to do—because he or she is typically closest to the team's customer—is to show up at the team meetings and either confirm or reconfirm that the shared promise is still relevant and satisfying the team's customer. So every meeting starts with saying something like this to the team: "I just spoke with Susan last week, and if we produce these results, she's still fully onboard. That's exactly what she wants from us." Or a team leader might say to the team, "Until you hear otherwise from me, please know that I'm checking with Susan regularly and we're on track. Okay?" That's the first thing the team leader needs to do always.

The other most important role of the team leader is managing the team's conversations. The leader doesn't need to lead each conversation and shouldn't dominate or be speaking more than anyone else. In fact, ideally, the leader speaks the least in team meetings. Managing the conversation means the leader is making sure that the team stays connected to the conversation that the team needs to have.

For example, in an action meeting, the team leader says, "All right, let's have a conversation about the status of all our promises. Let's go around, and we'll start with you, John. What's the status of your three promises?"

And John says, "The first promise is on track. Second promise is also on track. Third promise is a red flag; we're in trouble."

And someone next to John says, "What's going on?"

And John starts to describe the problem, and immediately the team gets into a heated conversation about what to do about this problem. That's actually not the right conversation at the right time. Getting sidetracked to solve problems that arise during an action meeting is exactly what derails the conversation. Right now we're going over the status of our promises. And so people in team meetings get frustrated because we get derailed and try to solve a problem, and then the time is up, and we never even talked about all the other promises, and we don't know what's going on.

So the team leader needs to stay present and (especially those leaders that avoid conflict) have the courage to redirect the team by saying like, "Okay, John and Bill, can you work on this? And, John, I think you need to make a request for another meeting when we can do this. But now is not the time because we're going over the status of all the promises. That's why we're here." Whatever conversation the team is having, the team leader is in charge of making sure we stay in that conversation. This can be really hard because the team leader often is the first one who gets sucked into solving problems.

At the end of the day, the team leader owns and consistently reports the status of the shared promise to the team's customer. When leaders embrace these responsibilities, teams stay motivated and focused and work more efficiently.

As a leader, a great way to foster teamwork and show appreciation is with what I call positive feedback minus one. Some of the best positive feedback I've ever seen in organizations occurs when the team leader has his or her boss give the team or team member positive feedback. For example, I am the team leader; Karen works for me; and my boss is Lisa. So I go to Lisa, and I say, "Lisa, I want you to know that last month Karen not only doubled her number, but she got incredible feedback from one of our clients because she went way beyond and they're super happy with her." Then Lisa either pulls Karen in or calls Karen and says, "Hey, Karen, I just want you to know that I spoke with Craig, and I heard what you did with that customer and your numbers, and I'm really proud of you and thank you very much." That can be more important to a person's career and strengthen their loyalty more than a financial bonus. And it takes two minutes.

TEAMWORK

High-performing teams trust each other, and they work on trust. They have very clear agreed upon behavioral standards. And they not only live them but they revisit and talk about how they're doing as a team typically every quarter. So I see really high-performing teams meet every three months, even if it's just for half an hour, where they don't talk operations or promises. They only talk about how they're doing as a team. And sometimes those are brought into team off-site meetings where I'm involved. We work on how well they're living their standards and looking for breakdowns to fix. And high-performing teams have the missing conversations. They are really good at seeing conversations that aren't happening. And they have enough trust, care, and courage to have the conversation quickly.

It's unfortunately rare that I see teams in good shape, to be honest. But I recently worked with a team that was leaps and bounds above most I see. I was brought in by my client—the team leader—by videoconference to observe a team meeting. So I introduced myself and then went on mute while they conducted their normal meeting. And while there is always room for improvement, this team was really good at listening to each other. They were really good at debating issues without making it personal. They stayed in the conversations that they needed to have. They were good at making decisions and clarifying who owned what and what the next steps would be. These are fundamentals, and yet I find that they're missing in so many organizations. So many team meetings that I observe are just a lot of people talking about stuff, and nothing actually gets decided; nothing actually clears up. So no wonder people dread going to another meeting.

But teamwork is just like everything else in leadership. It's a performance art. It requires practice. It requires understanding. It requires having conversations. It requires alignment. And what's unbelievable to anyone who's ever been part of a highly performing, effective team is that it is the most fun you've ever had when it works.

9

Learn to Celebrate, Renew, and Declare You Are Enough

Some of the most common challenges and topics I work on with clients are overwhelm, stress, and even burnout. At very senior levels, not only do leaders believe they "should" be able to handle all of it, but in addition, they rarely have places to share their concerns, fears, and deep challenges when dealing with such complex issues, lack of time, and what seems like a never-ending flow of requests and problems.

As part of a recent coaching session with a client, we looked at his calendar together and noticed something I see all the time. Week after week, his days were divided into half-hour slots, one meeting after the other, all day, every day. No matter how often I see it, a calendar booked this solid seems unbelievable, undoable. And I just said, "When do you have time to think?" The man smiled an uncomfortable smile and shrugged. But what could he say? This is the world many of us live in.

One of my clients, when they send calendar invites, you get your choice of twenty-five minutes or fifty. They purposely have meetings that only last fifty minutes because they realized that if the meeting lasts for an hour, you don't have any time in between to go to the bathroom, have a glass of water, or even breathe and prepare for what's next. Those are the basics. But studies have shown it takes fifteen minutes to emotionally shift out of one conversation and get ready for the next, which means all these meetings are happening and people aren't even ready. That's just one example; there are other strategies you can use to ease overwhelm.

CELEBRATE

A common denominator in leaders and especially in their teams is that everyone goes a thousand miles an hour. And by the time the team actually produces a significant result, reaches a milestone, or has a success, they're so busy working on the next four things that no one ever stops to acknowledge what just happened. When I ask leaders and teams, "Are you celebrating successes?" the answer I hear most of the time is, "We don't ever celebrate." Unless it's someone's birthday, most teams don't acknowledge any milestones.

Celebration is one of the missing pieces in leadership and in teams. When we don't take time to acknowledge our accomplishments, people begin to feel like they are not appreciated. When this happens, the entire mood of the team is affected, and instead of living in ambition, excitement, and curiosity (great moods for producing team results), the team is often living in frustration, ambivalence, or even resignation. They start to feel like it doesn't really matter what they do; nothing is going to change around here. When I talk to people about why they're dissatisfied, one of the main reasons is lack of acknowledgment.

One reason I think leaders don't celebrate is because they're afraid that if we acknowledge that we reached a goal, everyone will say, "We did it; we're done," and run out of the building. And yet that fear isn't substantiated at all. It doesn't make any sense. So I often say that the one thing we celebrate once a year is the fact that we didn't die. I'm kidding, but what's interesting is for adults on our birthdays, the celebration, in addition to presents and cake and loved ones, is often a chance to reflect on the year and what's coming next. And that's exactly what is missing in organizations and teams.

Celebrating success doesn't have to be a party; the simple act of acknowledging that we just did a good job and celebrating that for a few minutes can actually do more good for morale than a pay raise. We need to say, "You know what? We said we would produce this result, and we did. And that's great, and we're satisfied. Now, let's go to the next one." As human beings, our ability to take the time to reflect on what just happened and what we learned and appreciate what has been accomplished helps us stay focused on the bigger picture and foster positive and productive moods for the team each day. What would it look like on your team if you built in a new practice to share one thing learned and one thing you were proud of after every major project ends, or even once a month in team meetings?

RENEW

Every time you get on an airplane, when the attendants are going over the emergency procedures, they always say make sure your oxygen mask is secure before helping anyone else. You can't be much help if you can't breathe. This idea of taking care of yourself first before you take care of others translates to the workplace as well. If a leader is going to lead, he or she has to be able to breathe.

Renewal means taking time for you to rest, regroup, and think. This could be anything from playing golf to taking a yoga class to spending the afternoon watching television. It's about doing whatever you need to do to feel balanced and relaxed. Celebrating anniversaries with your spouse and making it to all your kid's games don't count; I'm talking about you and time for yourself. No one wants to be the dead hero, and when you're working your butt off and putting in extra hours, even if you feel like you can handle it, it's not sustainable.

We all know how important renewal is; we've all read the studies, and we've all heard stories about stressed-out people who snap. We also know that when our boss or someone that works for us is not taking care of him- or herself, it makes us very nervous. The need for renewal makes perfect sense. And even though we know this, leaders are simply not practicing renewal enough or sometimes not at all.

When we begin, so many of my clients don't have renewal practices, and they are doing the best they can to keep from drowning. The mind-set I see most is that they don't need it. People think, "I'm really good at keeping all the balls in the air, so I'm just going to keep moving forward." But when we do this, burnout is inevitable. People who don't practice renewal for themselves struggle to stay healthy, especially on vacations because they're so used to running on empty that the minute their bodies slow down a little, they get sick. And I don't mean just once; this happens for people all the time, every vacation.

I'll connect with my client after they had their summer vacations and ask, "How was it?"

"Well, you know, I spent the first four days in bed with a fever."

When I start to dig, I find out it happens for these clients every time. I have a number of clients that suffered through this until we could build a practice around renewal. And I know how it feels because it was my life for a long time too.

When I left corporate and went on my own, I made some big decisions about designing my life to be satisfied because I could easily have fallen into the same rhythm. So I've created renewal practices. I have at least one or two weekdays every month where I block the entire day, months in advance. I say no to every client. My family knows that it's my day as well. And those are my renewal days. I take the entire day to do whatever I need to do to renew. Typically, for me it's going to the golf course or taking a walk. Sometimes it's Netflix and PJs. Whatever it is, it's what I need. And I have seen a huge impact in my ability to be focused and present and committed at work because I'm taking better care of myself. Even though I used to be the guy who got sick all the time, I don't get sick anymore. Amazingly, I don't even get colds. It's quite miraculous. I spend my life getting on airplanes, flying across the world to be with teams for two and three days, and even though I may have jinxed it by writing this, I've never canceled anything. But it's not because I'm a martyr; it's because I'm healthy. I'm happy, and I'm satisfied.

I was talking to a banker on a flight about how I block a few days each month, and he said that he couldn't block weekdays because he worked in a corporate environment. But he did take a couple of days every month creating ad hoc conversations with people in his office. He worked with his assistant to keep his schedule for those days clear of meetings and calls and had been doing it for about six months. This was the top guy in a major Swiss bank. And for him, not having a schedule of back-to-back meetings on those days was incredibly renewing.

If you're in a leadership role, you're responsible for creating a path for others, and therefore you're responsible for creating practices to take care of yourself. When I say take care of yourself, there are all sorts of levels. For example, people often say they keep their weekends for themselves. But that's not actually true for most people because that's when we take care of our families. When I'm working with my clients, we look at ways to build actual time in your calendar and give your renewal the same importance that you would give to a meeting with a client or with your boss. It doesn't matter how you spend that time. I have some clients who read, go for a walk, go to the gym, or get a massage. It doesn't matter what you do, as long as it helps you recharge. What's most important is that you build a sustainable renewal practice. So that on a Tuesday at 2:00 p.m., for an hour, you close your door, you're not available, your calendar is blocked, and you're actually doing something that renews you. I have clients who, more and more, build renewal into their professional life, and the results have been outstanding.

What I'm proposing is not that radical, and it doesn't even need to be that big of a step. Could you start by blocking thirty minutes every week for no one but you? What would that look like? In my experience, every time, if a person can get there and really dedicate the thirty minutes to themselves, it pretty quickly becomes easy to make it sixty, and then we keep going.

We have plenty of evidence in the world of executives having breakdowns, getting burned out, feeling overwhelmed, and making huge mistakes because they're going too fast. I see it everywhere I go. You don't need to be shipwrecked, have a major disaster in your life, or quit your job. But you have every right—even the responsibility—to take better care of yourself so that you can take better care of others. Have the courage to renew yourself. Your career depends on it. So pull out your calendar, and schedule your time. And then practice giving yourself permission by saying to yourself, "Renewal and space is just as important as being busy or more."

YOU ARE ENOUGH

People have no trouble finding ways to renew. But we can't help feeling like we don't deserve it. How can I possibly say no to someone who needs to meet with me, so that I can take better care of myself?

Putting the time on the calendar is one thing; learning how to not feel guilty about it is the real challenge. The greatest obstacle to renewal is not so much about the calendar. It's not tactical; it's emotional. Most people I work with, if we go back to the impostor syndrome, have a story about how, with everything else they do, they couldn't possibly take an hour for themselves. They don't feel like they deserve to renew. But how could you not? If you don't, everything could come crashing down.

The impostor syndrome, which drives so much behavior in organizations, is based in fear of not being enough. The story that I see over and over in so many people is, "I'm not enough: I'm not smart enough; I'm not fast enough; I'm not analytical enough; I'm not strategic enough; I'm not enough of a leader." And if we don't feel like we're enough, then we don't feel like we deserve breaks and time to renew.

The most powerful way to overcome this is shifting the story. What if I actually realize I am enough? I'm not a superhero. I'm not perfect, I'm going to make mistakes, and yet I can show up at work, committed to doing my best and totally committed to the belief that I am enough. If you want to be a satisfied leader instead of an unsatisfied leader, you have to believe you are enough.

There's a direct correlation between the belief that I'm enough and practicing being satisfied—one leads directly to the other. One of my teachers once told me about a minister of finance from Bolivia, who was indigenous to that country. He said the credo of his tribe of people differed from that of the Europeans, particularly the Spanish, who colonized South America in the 1500s. And he said basically that the Spaniards were driven by the search for a better life—that's why they traveled across the ocean and justified the atrocities they inflicted on the native people they encountered. Unfortunately, you can justify almost anything for the pursuit of a better life. But if you're always looking for a better life, you actually can't be satisfied, ever. The minister of finance explained that his people, going back centuries, were different. Instead of pursuing a better life, they pursued a good life. Hearing that was helpful to me because I realized I needed to practice being satisfied. Like many of the clients I work with, I didn't have the ability to declare satisfaction. It's always the story of, "Yeah, but it could be better." Or, "We need to get there next."

Satisfaction is not saying, "I'm done forever." Satisfaction is saying, "This is enough; this is a job well done. We had a good day. I'm going to celebrate that. I'm going to take a moment to recharge my batteries; then I'm going to create some new promises, and I'm going to go work really hard and have fun." And doing it that way, all the flow comes from joy.

Often after working with leaders, over and over again I get feedback from their teams like, "Wow. Clearly our boss has shifted. The work you did has made a big difference in their pace, how they interact with others, and so on." These practices are holistic. If someone can declare himself or herself enough and build renewal at work, of course, it has a huge impact at home too. Celebration and renewal and declaring that you're enough are all the pathways into finding deeper satisfaction in all aspects of life.

10

Learn to Identify What You Care About and Design Everything to Take Care of That

As I've mentioned, there are two extremes when we talk about leaders, and all of us fit somewhere in that spectrum. And whether you're the kind of leader who is directive and not listening, or the kind of leader who is empathetic but avoiding conflict, the best path I have discovered toward the middle starts with the question, "What do I care about?" It may seem odd to think that care has anything to do with corporate life, organizations, and leadership. And yet I've learned that we as human beings don't fully commit to anything unless it takes care of what we care about.

With one of my clients, we often meet as a team at eight in the morning. And these executives come in, and they've already run for an hour or more and had a shower. They're all middle-aged and in incredible shape. And I look at them and can't believe they've been up since five and already gone running. When I ask them, "What makes you do that?" the answer is, "Well, I run every day," or, "I run five days a week, and it's just who I am." And when I question them further and ask why, they say something like, "Running brings me energy, makes me feel better, makes me more productive, and gives me a better sense of my appearance, or whatever it is." These people aren't out there running before the sun comes up because a boss told them they have to run, because their spouse said they should get in shape, or because someone else made them. Their commitment comes from something they care about.

When you think about times you've fully committed to anything—such as making a decision to change cities, to buy a home, to have a child, to change jobs, to fire someone—it wasn't because someone told you to do it. When you're making these huge decisions and being fully committed to that, I posit that's because it's taking care of something that you care about. This may happen consciously or unconsciously. And it's nondiscretionary; it happens whether or not we see it. But again, awareness brings choice. When you understand this and get more connected to what actually matters, it helps you make better decisions. It helps you drive your life instead of making you feel like life is living you.

So for me to fully commit to something, and more importantly, in order for people to follow me and bring their full commitment, I, as a leader, must get very clear on what I care about and what they care about. That's where the commitment comes from. And there's a difference between commitment and compliance. Compliance is, "Yes, ma'am. I'll do it because you told me to do it." That's not what we're looking for in leadership. In leadership, the Holy Grail is people who bring ownership and accountability. That comes from commitment. So I look at this person who's out running and I say, "Where does that commitment come from?" It comes from taking really good care of something that matters. So that person runs.

When a leader says, "I care about creating more collaboration. It really matters to me on the team," then this leader will constantly look for reasons to bring the team together, break down silos, listen more, and get the team outside of the office creating relationships. The leader makes these decisions because she cares about the team working together. Because then she doesn't have to do it herself. Because it's easier. Because it's more fun. Because it's more effective.

WHAT DO YOU CARE ABOUT?

One of the biggest questions that I have worked with personally for the last ten years and that I ask all my clients are these simple five words: "What do you care about?" In my own case, as someone who was a pleaser, who has to constantly work against that part of myself, this question created a huge breakdown for me because I had no idea. I was really good at knowing what everybody else cared about. But I didn't know what I cared about; I'd never thought about that. When I started to discover it, I realized a large part of my professional and personal life wasn't aligned at all. I wasn't taking care of what I cared about, which was why I was so dissatisfied. So I started to say no and began making changes and redesigning.

When I started my business, I realized one of the things that I cared about was putting my wife and my kids first, making them the first priority. But when I looked at my corporate life, I hadn't been doing that. The presentation was coming first, the project, or the team. My family got my attention after I was done with work. And so, when I started this business, I made some really clear decisions and created new standards. For example, I won't be gone more than one weekend in a row for work travel. And when my business took off, I had lots of opportunities to go from Spain to the United States, Latin America, and Asia and do multiple projects. People would hire me and say, "Can you spend this week in this city? And then the following week, we're going to go to a different city," which, as a contractor, is incredibly enticing. They were offering to pay me a whole bunch, and I was basically selling all these days together. And yet what it meant was that I would be gone for three weekends in a row. This would have killed my family because weekends are for us. So I said no. And I told them why, truly believing when I was saying no that I would lose the client and probably the momentum of my business. The client was surprised. But they respected it, said, "No problem," gave me more work, and never asked me again to be gone two weeks in a row. I think they actually respected me more, and it reminded them to reconsider their own commitments.

Another one of my practices is every single Friday, I ask myself again, "What do I care about?" and come back to my answer. I have it written in a Word document, and every Friday I read it and consider whether or not I'm spending my time focused on promises in life and my profession that aligns with what I care about. My life is like going on a river raft; there are rapids, and there are times that it's slower. But I know that once a week I'm going to park my boat, get out on dry land, take off my wet clothes, lie down on the beach, look up, and ask myself, again, "Why am I in the river? Where am I going? What is it that actually matters? What is it that I care about, and am I this week taking care of what I care about? What's missing?" That's what I do every Friday, and it gives me the ability to get back in the boat and bring tremendous freedom and fun during the week. Because I know that on Friday, I'm going to get out, again, and check in. When I didn't do this, I'd get lost. All of a sudden, I'd realize years had gone by, and I didn't know what the hell I was doing. Now I get out of the river every week and make sure that I'm not missing something. So then the rest of the week, I can just go have fun in the river. I've found that when you do that every week, everything stays aligned. What's been amazing is by creating a life and a job that's aligned with what I care about, life gets really good. And in all aspects, I have more fun. I have more freedom. I make more money. I create more value.

Sometimes what we care about has levels. When I ask clients the question, we get to the obvious quickly. I care about my spouse. I care about my children. I care about my health. Okay. And yet there's always more on a deeper level. I encourage you, and what I've done is to look at where you truly are committed.

For example, when I started reflecting and making a list of what I care about, I wrote down making money, which is a weird thing to add to a list that also includes making my wife and kids my first priority; learning, growing, bringing meaning to my life; and supporting leaders in becoming more successful and more satisfied. It didn't make any sense and felt banal. So I explored why I care about money and realized that I didn't care about it at all. I care about sustaining a lifestyle. I care about buying a new computer the same day one breaks and saying yes to the more expensive travel location for our vacation. I've lived through times in my life where big expenses like that were difficult if not impossible. I don't care about mansions and Ferraris, but I care about being able to live in what abundance looks like for me. The question of what you care about is really a doorway into learning about yourself.

Once you understand what you care about, you can design your life and your work to take care of that. I recently did some work with a client who was extremely successful and extremely dissatisfied. We had a conversation about what he cared about, and I asked him, "Given what you care about, what does your life and your work look like if you're taking full care of what you care about?" Notice I didn't ask him what kind of job he wanted or what company he wanted to work for. We have to consider the attributes of the life and work we want. How much time are you devoting to work? What kind of time are you spending with your family? What is your relationship with your team and boss? So we don't know where this will end up, but we're beginning to say, "This is exactly what it looks like if I'm taking care of what I care about." And when you're really clear on what you want and need, you know what to look for. So he went out and found it. The end of the story was this person courageously left the company that he was working in without another job lined up. But after a very little time, because he knew what he was looking for, he found a new role that was built on the foundation of care and looked exactly like what he described in our conversations.

One of the common denominators of dissatisfied leaders is that when I really get them into a safe conversation, they will share over and over again, "I'm stuck. I'm a victim. I'm doing everything I can not to drown." They talk about being in overwhelm and not being in control and not making decisions, just taking life as it comes without anything ever getting any better. But when people start designing life to take care of what they care about, I've seen people shift their mood from victim, resignation, and resentment into ambition, curiosity, and hope. And when you shift your mood, you have all sorts of new options.

If there's one question that I'd like every reader to take and apply for the rest of his or her life, it's this: What do I really care about? It's amazing that we're not teaching this question in third grade, because I don't think there's anything more important to know and apply to life's decisions. First, build the foundation by knowing what matters. And from there, go design. Then you'll begin to feel like you're living your life, you're making decisions, and you're designing what it's going to look like as opposed to just doing the best you can with what's thrown at you. That's the big shift.

COMMITMENT COMES FROM CARE

To be a great leader—to declare a future that other people will commit to—you need to be really good at getting their commitment. And the road to their commitment starts with care.

Everyone wants results. We want the X million in yearly sales, the increase in shareholder value, or the team to finally work well together. So how do you get it? Well, we know results come from action. We have to get people to take action, and we have to take action ourselves. Everyone knows that. So part of leadership is getting people to take action to get the results. But what inspires action?

Bob Dunham, who taught me the care question, has a model that he calls the anatomy of action. The model looks like this:

CARE
↓
CONVERSATIONS
↓
COMMITMENT
↓
ACTION
↓
RESULTS

To develop the model, Bob explored the question of how to inspire action and get results for years and learned that action comes from commitment. Remember that commitment is not compliance. It's embodied commitment. So where does that come from? How do I get commitment? And Bob discovered that commitment is always born in conversations—conversations that I'm having with myself, with another person, or with others. As a leader, I need to get better and better at conversations through practice. Because if leadership is a performance art, which we've talked about before, I can't get good at it without practice. Then at the very top, what sits above everything else in the anatomy of action, is care. Because human beings actually commit when it connects to their care, when it takes care of what they care about. You talk to them, you tell them what matters to you and why, and you ask them questions. So it's not that we all have to care about the same things; it's that I, as a leader, need to get really clear about what I care about. And if I want the commitment from someone else, I'm going to connect to his or her care. I need to understand what matters to them, because that's where I'll get their commitment.

DESIGNING YOUR LIFE AND WORK AROUND CARE

As a leader, how do you get better at understanding what your team cares about? This is important, but it's also a little awkward because you can't exactly come out and ask, "So what do you care about?" Most people won't feel comfortable answering. It needs to start with the leader. Your job is to declare a future that your team will commit to, not that they will comply with. I don't want my team to say, "Yes, sir. Yes, Craig. Whatever you say, I'll go do it." That's not what I'm looking for. The leader has to describe to his or her team what that future looks like and why it's important and then ask each team member, "What are you going to bring? What's your commitment going to look like?" You want your people to get excited about being creative, bringing their own ideas, creating their own promises, and contributing to the vision. And you want them to bring specific promises—it's not just, "I will do my best," but rather the tangible, measurable outcome or key result and by when.

From there, you listen and get to know your team members. If someone who works for me cares about recognition, as an example, that's more important than a pay rate. Letting people know that I appreciate what they've done and celebrating their results is what really matters. That's where I'm going to get their commitment; that's where I'm going to get their creativity, their trust, their loyalty. That's where it comes from. And I've learned the best way that I can get good at listening to what other people care about is by starting with myself.

As a leader, your ability to share not only what the future looks like for your team to succeed but also why it matters to you, why you care, will promote trust. And the ability to get team members to feel safe and trust you and connect is one of the missing recipes to success in leadership. That's what we're not being taught in the MBA or in college. And yet that's what this is about. That's how human beings bring their commitments. Because it is based on trust. It is based on connection.

Leaders declare a future even though it has never been declared before; it doesn't exist. Leaders lead other people into the unknown. When you can anchor yourself in what you care about and what others care about, things that weren't possible before become possible.

Conclusion

Leadership is demanding, difficult work. And most leaders are so busy, they never stop for long enough to realize that they're not supposed to know all this stuff. Many find comfort in the fact that they're not alone in their struggles. We all have areas that could be improved. We could all use a timeout every once in a while. By better understanding the leader's role and what great leadership looks like, you gain the perspective to find missing conversations and other issues that are preventing you and your team from succeeding at the highest levels.

The people I work with are very smart and very successful. And they're very good at producing results when that's what they focus on. The thing is, they tend to focus on hitting a number, not on building standards, increasing collaboration, listening better, building trust. All these soft skills are the building blocks to people working together effectively and hitting the higher numbers. Leading a group of human beings aligned and working together in a collaborative fashion to produce a specific result requires a totally different skill set. When you take a deep breath and create some new practices and focus on these pieces, then, guess what? You'll get better, quickly. And things will go well because, if you're like my clients, you're super smart. You just haven't been working on this.

Give yourself permission to be a beginner and to be really grateful for everything that you've achieved and those who have helped you. Then pick one or two areas of focus from the book, and start practicing right now in your work. Every time I do work with a team, every time I do work with a client, there is no other answer. Just pick one thing. For instance, have a missing conversation. For instance, go out and see where trust is broken and see if you can rebuild it. For instance, say no. For instance, listen a little longer in the next conversation. For instance, consider for yourself what you care about and what really matters. For instance, go and look for complainers and victims, and help them make better requests and get better promises. None of this will be that valuable or that interesting or certainly that relevant unless you, the reader, make it real through practice. This is not meant to be a theory, something to learn and create a slide and put it away. It is meant to be like the beginning of how to speak Spanish. And the only way you're going to speak Spanish is through practice. That's it. That's the secret.

Trying a new practice in itself is an exercise in the unknown, because you don't know what's going to happen. So it's uncomfortable, and we don't like this, and we're not very good at it, and we don't even know if it's going to work. One of the things that happens often with my clients is they'll say, "But if I do this, I'm going to lose my edge and forget how to make plans and bring structure."

And my response is, "No, you're not." And I invite them to go test it. Don't believe me. Go take a look. We are what we practice. And if we've practiced something for years, it's not going to go away. Just because you put your focus, your energy, and your attention on a new practice doesn't mean you lose something. You don't forget how to ride a bike when you learn how to drive a car.

I could name so many clients who have reported back to me that just limiting the amount of times they interrupt someone changed everything. This one small practice has profound results. Pick any practice from any chapter, and try it. If saying no is an issue for you, can you, in the next six weeks, find ways to push back and then notice the impact? That's it. I'm talking about little things.

In the next conversation that you have, let the person speak for ten seconds without doing anything but listening. Just stay with them a little longer and then ask a question from curiosity, rather than tell them the answer you think they're looking for. Just try that and see what happens.

Can you walk into the next meeting, just bringing the question: What do I actually need to be satisfied? Can you get a promise from someone? Just stay with the conversation until someone shows up with a promise, and then notice what happens.

Can you look the next time that you distrust someone and realize that that sense of distrust is your assessment and not theirs? Can you recognize that you're responsible for the distrust? And can you begin to break down the four areas, sincerity, reliability, confidence, and care; look at where exactly the distrust is coming from; and figure out a conversation that you could have with that person to potentially build or rebuild trust? Can you try it?

My challenge to you is choose whichever one of these areas of leadership that made the most sense, had the most relevance, struck a chord, reminded you the most of where you're stuck. And in that, build your first practice. That's it. Go practice, notice the impact, and then keep going. These are the fundamental skills that actually make leaders better. I wish you all the best, and don't forget to keep asking for help.

Acknowledgments

This book never would have happened without an amazing support network, and so I would like to thank my wife, Eva, for her contribution and support. When I went to her and said, "I think there's something to this coaching thing; I think this is what I want to do," her initial reaction was, "You know, that sounds like something that works in the States, sweetheart. And it sounds like a great hobby, but we actually have to make a living and support our family." And as much as it scared her and shook her, she is the strongest person I've ever met, and within days she'd shifted the whole idea for herself. She came to me and said, "I know you. I know if you don't make a successful business within two months, you're going to get completely frustrated. But that's unrealistic. We've got money saved, and it's going to be okay. So take an entire year, do it the right way, and we'll be fine." And she never shifted. Since then I've had her unconditional support. She's the driver behind my decisions and my partner in all that is this life.

Right there with us have been our sons, David, Daniel, and Josh; Mom; Dad; and Rick. Merche, Josesteban and Helena. Thank you.

Toward the end of my three-year master's program, Bob Dunham—my teacher, mentor, and coach—called me and said there were two new students in the program, and he wanted me to be their coach. I'd never coached anyone before, and so I responded, "I'm not a coach."

But he said, "I think you are." This moment, it was as if he and I were standing on a pier out on the bay. The water around us was choppy and intimidating, and he was telling me to jump in. I didn't know how to swim, but he encouraged me to do it anyway.

And when I jumped in the water, I realized I was a fish. That's how big a deal it was for me. I just trusted him that I could do this and not even really knowing anything, I just jumped in and realized, "Of course I can do this. In fact, I can do this a lot easier than nine out of ten things that I'm trying to do for the last twenty-five years." So in many ways, Bob, you were a huge influence in me taking this step.

To Kim Marie—where I have gone each week for the last nine years for reality checks, healing, learning, and friendship—thank you.

Libby, Christa, Juan Carlos, Michael—you are amazing teachers and supporters, and you are a gift in my professional and personal life.

Steven, thank you for calling me that day, years ago; telling me about the coach you'd been working with; and saying, out of the blue, "Craig, I think you should do this for a living."

Rich, thank you for over twenty-five years of friendship and unofficial coaching. You keep me honest by always asking if there is a "pero" behind my declaration of how well things are going.

Gema, Fito, Bernardo, Jacinto, Jim, Rafa, Víctor, Chris, Kirsten, Robert, Leah, Matt, Derek, Alfredo, Larry, Leah, Natalia, Mish and Punit—you have all contributed over these years to my learning, my growth, and my ability to keep choosing the most valuable path for me.

Of course, I want to thank all my clients. It has been a privilege to support you and to learn with you.

37474411R00063

Printed in Poland
by Amazon Fulfillment
Poland Sp. z o.o., Wrocław